BOAT FISHING

Boat Fishing

Mike Millman
Richard Stapley & John Holden

The Crowood Press

First published in 1985 by
THE CROWOOD PRESS LTD
Ramsbury, Marlborough
Wiltshire SN8 2HR

This paperback edition 1991

British Library Cataloguing in Publication Data

Millman, Mike
    Boat fishing.
    1. Saltwater fishing
    I. Title
    799.1'6   SH457
    ISBN 1 85223 685 X

All photographs by John Holden, except on pages
16, 44, 46, 51, 54, 79, 80, 87, 89, 105, 106 and 109
courtesy Mike Millman Photo Services.

Typeset by Inforum Ltd, Portsmouth
Printed in Great Britain by Hartnoll Ltd,
Bodmin, Cornwall

Contents

Foreword

Sea angling boats ply for hire from every port and harbour in Britain. Some cater for the passing holiday trade: mackerel fishing, half-day charters for general bottom fishing in the bay and tourist-style shark angling aimed directly at holiday makers with time on their hands and only a fleeting interest in fishing. Turn up at the quay, hand over your cash and climb aboard. It is a lighthearted introduction to the fringes of real sea angling and probably encourages thousands of newcomers to investigate the more serious side of the sport.

Look around the same harbour as dawn breaks and you will discover the real world of sea fishing. Fast workboats, trawlers and launches wait alongside while parties of oilskinned anglers load their own tackle aboard. Sometimes an entire fleet opens throttles and heads from port in a haze of diesel smoke. These are professional charter boats that spend all day at sea. Some run 40 miles (25km) out to deep sea wrecks which provide a bonanza of pollack, conger eels, coalfish and ling; perhaps a ton of fish between a dozen anglers who end the day exhausted. Other boats head for offshore sandbanks and reefs, home of bass, rays, cod and tope.

Watching from the harbour wall, you probably feel a complete outsider. Yes, it is a close-knit scene. Fishermen and charter craft operators never seem to have much in common with either the yachting fraternity or the public in general.

I suppose we do strike outsiders as unapproachable. There seems to be a silence of conspiracy, an unwillingness to mix with the outsider. The same is true of every club, every pastime, sport and hobby. Yet once the ice is broken you will find that boat fishermen, like anglers the world over, are a happy bunch – friendly, welcoming and actually enthusiastic to share their pastime with you. So forget about our growly facade, come along and join us in this fast growing sport.

1 Getting started

The club scene is indispensable for would-be boat anglers, and without doubt the best introduction to our sport. Coming fresh into the club you can be sure that somebody will be happy to show you the ropes. Many clubs run special courses for beginners in which plenty of theory and practice soon put you above the freelance newcomer who has to work out every detail for himself. You learn more in a year than some anglers pick up in a lifetime. Above all, you enjoy better, cheaper and more frequent access to boats and boat-fishing.

Why is it better to fish with a club?

Besides sharing knowledge and tuition, clubs offer tremendous advantages in the sheer mechanics of getting to sea. There are thousands of fishing boats around Britain, and a significant proportion offer a pretty low standard of service and results. In most ports there are three or four boats that set the pace, half a dozen that come a close second in the race for fish, and a few tail enders who just cannot get it together. Some skippers try hard but lack the spark which sets top professionals apart. Some are rip-off merchants who never bother to find fish. Once at sea they drop anchor, lock themselves below and leave you to it.

Skippers with a reputation for service and results are booked throughout the season and frequently for years in advance. The only way to be sure of getting aboard some popular boats is by regular bookings, say, fortnightly or monthly. Clubs and groups of anglers are in a stronger negotiating position than an individual. Deposits are the rule these days, and you may have to order and pay in advance for baits as well.

Charter boats normally sail for a set fee which does not vary according to the number of anglers on board. If the boat costs £60 a day, eight anglers going to sea pay £7.50 a head. Book the boat yourself and you pay the full £60. You may persuade some friends to go along, but you can seldom depend on it. Even if you are forced to cancel there is still the deposit to pay – and some skippers insist on the full charter fee as well, plus compensation for wasted bait.

A club is in a much stronger position. In return for a block booking of say, twelve trips in a year, a skipper may offer more favourable terms. At the very least his fee will remain static for the whole booking period. Any healthy club can muster a full crew every trip; if not, it is standard practice for the club itself to stand the loss from its own funds, or at least to subsidise the financial shock to the anglers who do sail. As a member of the club you enjoy fishing at bargain rates, particularly if the club also arranges group travel between home and port.

The only drawback is that you may have to draw lots or join a waiting list for a trip out. On the other hand, you lose nothing because as a freelance angler you would never have secured a booking on that boat anyway. The same applies to bait orders: a club that enlists its own digger is sure of better service and keener prices than you would find by wandering into a tackle shop on the off-chance of a few worms.

Alternatives do exist. Groups of free-lance anglers band together to book a charter boat. Sometimes it develops into a regular arrangement; more often one or two people leave the group, costs per head rise, or the trip may be cancelled when three or four anglers suddenly drop out. Lost deposits and inflated prices aggravate the situation and the group disbands, usually having fallen out with the boat-man as well. On the other hand, some groups stay together for years with never a complaint; much depends on the indi-viduals involved.

The problem of freelance anglers is rec-ognised by booking agencies which act as intermediaries between individuals and boatmen. When the agent has enough names, he arranges a joint booking. The system can work well but frequently falls down because either you have to wait so long for a trip that you cancel, or you find yourself on board the worst vessel in the fleet, in which case you vow never to visit that port again.

Skippers themselves may make up a party from a waiting list of individuals; and there are a few boatmen, usually based in busy resorts, who take each day as it comes, load up on the quayside and set sail when the party is complete. Pay-ment is a flat fee per head and if the necessary number fail to turn up the skip-per either sails regardless or may cancel. It is a cheap way to get to sea but none too reliable. Overall, the club system is best, with group arrangements equally good or a close second *if* you pick the right mates.

Why not buy your own boat?

Every boat fisherman dreams of his own craft. There is no greater sense of achieve-ment and freedom than to slip your moor-ings and motor out to sea after those elusive monster cod and bass. Even if you can afford to, do not rush into owning a fishing boat or even a dinghy until you have a sound background of seamanship. The sea is potentially dangerous at the best of times. A raw beginner at the helm of his own boat, untutored and without somebody to keep an eye on him, is a menace to himself and to the rescue ser-vices who may be called upon to save his skin.

Before you make any move towards boat ownership, do learn something about the sea itself and the types of craft most suit-able for sea fishing in your local waters. Clubs are the short cut to expertise, so join one with its own dinghy and small boat section where you will learn a great deal about boat fishing itself and benefit from club facilities – typically a dinghy com-pound, launching ramp and recovery winch. Better to be slow off the mark than quick and drowned.

How do you join a club?

There are thousands of fishing clubs in Britain. Some cover coarse, fly and salt-water fishing, others concentrate on one major branch of the sport. Within the salt-water associations are specialist clubs which narrow the field even more: mem-bers are keen on a single species like tope, bass and conger eels, or spend most of their time wreck fishing, rock fishing or tourna-ment casting.

Local clubs are the best starting point. Almost every town and village in the country supports a fishing club of some

Leaving port for a day on the reefs.

kind, even if it comprises only half a dozen members who meet in the pub three times a year. Do not make the mistake of discounting small clubs in favour of bigger, more prestigious organisations. Some of the keenest anglers prefer to fish with a few mates rather than within a hundreds-strong club (with its inevitable politics, committees and petty rules). Look around before you decide.

Most clubs are open to all applicants though there may be a limited number of members and thus a waiting list to join. Other clubs are an offshoot of a larger sports and social club. Again, membership may be open but could be restricted either to members of the parent club itself or, in the case of industry and the public services, to employees and their families. It is surprising how many would-be anglers working for big companies are unaware that their social club has a fishing section. Some of the bigger clubs own their own boats and coaches, and are extremely well supported with subsidised club facilities, competition prizes and cheap loans.

To locate independent clubs, look through local directories, check the personal and small ad. sections of the local press, and ask at the library or Citizen's Advice Bureau. The nearest Sports Council committee should be able to help, as will the National Federation of Sea Anglers, our leading organisation to which most major clubs are affiliated. Write to The Secretary, 26 Downsview Crescent, Uckfield, TN22 1UB. Closer to home, it is a fair bet that your favourite pub has its own fishing club – even if it is an informal arrangement.

How much does it cost to fish from a boat?

Working through a club or group, you pay less for your fishing than by booking independently or buying your own boat. It is hard to pin down an exact price list because boat fishing exists in so many forms. You may join a club which owns its own fleet of dinghies, in which case the cost of a day's fishing for three men in a boat is less than £2 each. All you pay for is petrol and overheads like storage, maintenance and insurance. Bigger club boats are charged accordingly, but the outlay is still less than you would expect on a commercial charter. As a member of a club with its own craft, be thankful – you can never find cheaper sport.

The typical bottom-fishing charter boat operating within 10 miles (16km) of port on an 8 hour trip pitches its rates somewhere in the £40–£80 bracket depending on the facilities, the skipper's reputation and the number of anglers who fish. Sharing the cost between the six, eight or even twelve anglers at sea, and adding on the cost of bait, you can expect to pay £5–£10 a trip. Add to that the price of replacing lost tackle, food and petrol . . . say £15 all-in for a day's sport depending how far you must travel from home to port, whether you share a car or drive alone.

It is no use pretending that boat fishing is cheap. Prices mentioned so far are the minimum payable for decent fishing. There is always a boatman prepared to take you out at bargain rates. Will he produce the fish? Is he licensed? Is the boat insured and fully equipped with navigational aids, radio, flares and liferafts? A couple of rough, fishless trips may persuade you to invest in a better deal next time.

Charter boats have traditionally operated at low rates, chiefly because anglers are reluctant to pay the full market price of good fishing, but partly because skippers themselves value their work and lifestyle above mere cash. Consequently the majority of charter boats just about break even. There is no flexibility in fishing arrangements: each trip lasts X hours; the boat burns no more than Y gallons of diesel oil. Within that framework the skipper can offer a neat package of good fishing and attractive rates. That keeps his diary full, pays his wages and covers overheads.

Wreck fishing 40 miles (60 km) offshore and 24–36 hour trips to distant sandbanks and tide races escalate the operating costs. Big, fast boats with twin turbo-charged diesels, radar, Decca Navigator, accommodation for crew and anglers and comprehensive survival equipment cost a fortune to buy, maintain and fuel. If you want the superior fishing they offer, prepare to pay a realistic fee. £200–£400 a trip would be in order, but many operators subsidise the rate by keeping most of the fish. Selling them, they make a better profit without crucifying the anglers. It is still an expensive sport. Plenty of keen anglers pay between £50 and £100 a head (boat, bait, accommodation, travelling) for the chance to drop on to a wreck bursting with specimen coalfish, ling, conger and pollack.

What is best for a beginner?

The basic 8 hour charter offers several advantages. It is long enough to produce good fishing, but does not stretch your limits. Few people take to boats like ducks to water. The hull rolls under your feet; you slip around on deck and make a mess of handling the rod and reel. It is no fun to be wet and cold – and most beginners lack the right clothing to ensure day-long comfort. And, above all, you might feel ill.

Chances are that you will be legering on a clean seabed from an anchored boat. It is far easier to fish a static trace than to drift across broken grounds, wrecks and reefs. Even if your party fishes uptide-style, you will soon get the hang of tackling up, baiting the hook and playing a fish. Almost certainly the skipper will cast for you if necessary and lend you suitable gear.

The seasickness angle? Nobody knows the effect the sea will have on him. Take heart that the majority of sea anglers are either never sick or seldom so. You might feel ill the first few times out in a rough sea, but feeling bad from time to time is an inevitable feature of boating. The worst you can do is worry about it.

A few unlucky souls just are not cut out for boat fishing. They are sick every time, calm or rough. The sight of a boat turns them green. If that is the case, the best course is to forget about boat fishing. There simply is no point trying to beat nature. Violent, prolonged sickness is distressing and potentially dangerous.

Protect yourself with seasickness pills, but, above all, develop a positive mental attitude. A great deal of sickness seems to be psychosomatic, the result of thinking yourself into feeling ill. Is that your own fear?

If it is, there is no mileage in saying 'I'm determined not to be ill'. It simply plays on your mind, and you spend all day thinking about *not* being sick . . . which mentally is just as bad as thinking about being ill. Say to yourself 'If I'm sick, I'm sick. Meanwhile, to hell with it, I'm going to enjoy fishing and learn all I can'.

A few homespun tricks may help – confidence boosters perhaps? Watch the horizon. Stand up rather than sit down. Stay away from the cabin and wheelhouse. Avoid engine fumes. Keep warm. Drink a little, eat a little. Apples and ginger are said to ward off queasiness – and they do reckon that a gallon of strong cider kills seasickness in anyone.

Some medical conditions and drugs may aggravate seasickness. The reverse also applies: being sick can seriously damage you physically and may interfere with medication levels. Dehydration alone is a severe risk. If you are under doctor's orders, check with him before you sail. Seasickness is not the end of it: the physical trauma of being tossed around all day may itself cause problems.

When should you buy your first set of tackle?

Buy no tackle until you know what kinds of boat fishing are available, and which of those you prefer. Species, water depth, fishing techniques and even the design of the charter boat influence your choice. Without some guidance and experience, you simply cannot judge which rod and reel to buy. Good tackle is expensive, and it is stupid to rush into the tackle shop unless you know that your cash (at least £100) is wisely invested. *Never* rely on the tackle dealer's advice unless you know him well enough to trust his judgement. For every good dealer, there is another who does not give a damn what you buy, as long as you buy plenty.

Why is so much tackle available?

Angling is a sport, not simply the means of hauling fish from the water. If it were a question of food alone, fishermen would be happy to dangle their baited hooks on a handline, which is actually a most effective weapon. There is the sporting element to be considered: the precision feel of a good rod and reel; easy accurate casting; sensitivity and fighting power calculated to match the size and strength of the species of fish you aim to lure. Mackerel are poor sport on shark tackle. Lightweight spinning rods, excellent for surface-feeding bass, are not strong enough to handle the pound of lead required to leger for skate in a tide race.

Baits and terminal tackle also vary according to species and conditions. Most of our fishing is with natural baits like fish strips, squid, worms and crabs presented on a paternoster or flowing trace anchored to the seabed with a lead sinker. Sometimes the tackle is lowered straight down over the side of the boat; in shallow, fast moving tides you may have to cast as far as possible from the hull.

Now and again, usually in deep water over reefs and wrecks, a string of artificial squid or a heavy metal pirk catch fish that ignore a static natural bait. No single outfit can possibly cope with such a variety of tasks. Some rods and reels are more versatile than others, but generally you need a special outfit for each technique and breaking strain of line.

2 Rods and reels for boat fishing

CHOOSING YOUR RODS

The performance of fishing rods is difficult to measure in scientific terms. Experienced anglers pick up a rod, bend the tip over by hand, flex the butt against the ground and make an instant, accurate assessment. What seems light for one angler may be a little too stiff for another even though they catch the same species of fish in identical conditions.

Whatever your personal preferences may be, remember that boat fishermen catch most fish on tackle balanced to the size of the species and how they feed. Suppose bass are feeding on sandeels washed along the seabed by a strong tidal current. The best bait is a lively sandeel presented on tackle just heavy enough to touch bottom but light enough to drift downstream to the waiting fish. 3oz of lead, 10lb line and a whippy 8–10ft rod makes a perfect outfit. Drop your bait over the side, pay out extra line . . . and wait for a big old bass to hit the sandeel. Then come the fireworks: bass usually weigh less than 10lb but they still fight hard on the right gear.

Suppose you chose to fish with a heavy boat rod and 50lb line. It takes at least 8oz of lead to sink the line itself. The sandeel on its trace hits the seabed and sticks fast, does not drift down to the feeding shoal.

So you catch nothing. Why not move the boat and drop the tackle straight down? Bass are shy fish which seldom tolerate a boat overhead. Even if they stayed around long enough to find your sandeel, were not deterred by the thickness of the line and actually did take the hook, you would do no more than crank them into the boat. No bass makes an impression on 50lb tackle. Where's the fun in it?

The tackle trade and leading organisations, led by the International Game Fishing Association, resolved to inject some sanity and stability into the muddled world of tackle specification as it relates to the fish we hook. They drew up a comparative system based on line breaking strain. Why pick line? It is easily measured and forms the backbone of the complete outfit, since its strength alone determines the useful limits of rod, reel and terminal rig.

From the competitive and record breaking points of view, the intricacies of the line class system hold little interest and value for British anglers. However, it is important when you choose a new rod and reel: most British and foreign manufacturers design and build boat rods roughly to conform with IGFA ratings.

12, 20, 30 and 50lb class are of special relevance to our boat fishing. They are more correctly measured in kilograms, but even the official body runs a dual measuring system simply because American anglers, who account for the overwhelming majority of line-class fishing, resist the

shift to metric. It has little following here either: just try asking your tackle dealer for 6kg line and a matching rod.

Use the line class system for convenient comparisons between rods and to draw up a league table of tackle weight for particular species of fish. With those yardsticks, you can select a rod, reel and line that give the sporting outfit for your favourite fish. It is not the perfect solution, but at least prevents disastrous mistakes like buying a shark rod to catch whiting and dabs.

LINE CLASS   SPECIES OF FISH

12lb Bass, whiting, dogfish, plaice, dabs, common eels, smoothhounds.
20lb Tope, cod, rays, turbot, pollack.
30lb Tope, big cod, ling, big pollack.
50lb Sharks, halibut, conger.

Increase the line class one step for deep water and fast tides which demand heavier than normal weights. *Increase* for obstructed marks like wrecks and pinnacle rocks unless you are particularly skilful. *Decrease* the line class for extra sport in easy waters and open ground or where the fish run smaller than usual.

MOST USEFUL ALL-ROUND OUTFITS FOR GROUND FISHING:

SHALLOW – MEDIUM DEPTH WATER, CLEAN GROUND, MODEST TIDES . . . 20lb CLASS

DEEP WATER, FASTER TIDES, MIXED BOTTOM . . . 30LB CLASS
It is assumed you will be fishing on the drift or from an anchored boat, without

casting away from the hull. Tackle for uptide casting is essentially different and will be discussed separately.

WHAT DO YOU LOOK FOR IN A LINE CLASS BOAT ROD?

Line class tackle is based on the traditional boat rod design of glass-fibre tip and detachable handle. Overall length varies roughly in step with poundage. 7.5 – 8.5ft is suitable for the 12lb and 20lb classes; 30–50lb rods are better kept around the 7ft mark which provides a better leverage ratio when you haul on the line.

Most boat rods are made from ordinary hollow fibreglass, a tough material which withstands a good deal of abuse and does not suffer from prolonged exposure to corrosive saltwater. The action of the blank (that is, the way it bends under load) is usually medium-fast, an ideal balance between easy handling and efficiency. For the moment, do not be concerned with more exotic rod materials, among them graphite and boron.

It is important that the handle be stiff enough to channel plenty of muscle power to the tip. Even light 12lb rods benefit from a substantial handle. Butts of flimsy glass-fibre absorb much of your effort, produce a 'soggy' feeling and are liable to break without warning. Thick-walled glassfibre, high-tensile aluminium alloy and straight grained wood (ash or hickory) are acceptable. Never compromise on the butt quality of the heavier rods: should a 50lb rod break under full load, splinters of metal, glass or wood will stab you in the belly.

Even lightweight fishing strains the reel seat. Snap-lock clips and weak screw

(Opposite) A full range of line class rods are essential for specialist fishing, but to begin with, choose an outfit in the 20–30lb range.

Rod blanks suffer an enormous amount of punishment, so make sure you buy a quality product with full manufacturer's guarantee.

fittings are useless on a boat rod. Choose the conventional chromed brass reel seat, the new Fuji FPS carbon-fibre/stainless steel seat or an equivalent. The butt and tip of the rod may be jointed under the reel seat, in which case you are better off choosing a rod fitted with the Modalock ferrule/reel seat, which, though heavy, is strong and reliable. Otherwise, pick a spigoted blank and butt, which do not require reinforcement from the reel seat itself.

All major tackle companies offer a range of conventional line-class boat rods. No end of rods conform to the basic design as far as length, power and blank/tip construction are concerned. You will probably need to choose from a shortlist of a dozen, all potentially suitable but diffe-

rent in both finish and price. Before making your decision, examine the rod rings, for they are the weak point of any rod. It is far better to have a modest blank and excellent rings than a superb blank with substandard fittings. In fact, it is sometimes better to build your own rod; then you can be sure of the best combination of blank, handle and accessories.

Fuji's aluminium oxide rings are excellent for 12, 20 and 30lb rods. There are several designs to choose: BNHG and BSHG for the lighter rods; low set rings in toughened cradles for the heavy tackle. British-made Seymo rings are equally good; Daiwa's stainless steel Dynaflo ring is suitable for 12 and perhaps 20lb fishing but not really man enough for the 30lb.

Ordinary rod rings like those listed are fine for all-round work but do not stand up to long term heavy fishing. When tension rises much beyond 20lb, line tends to stick in the ring. Roller rings are the answer for 30lb rods used at their limit, and for routine fishing with 50lb class rods. Mildrum and Aftco are a popular choice. Be wary of Oriental copies which collapse under the strain.

Standard tip rings are safe enough on 12 and 20lb rods. Heavy blanks are better served by tip rollers, which are mandatory on any rod to be used with wire line. Again, it pays to aim for a quality fitting even though it costs more. Tip rings and rollers absorb more strain than any other ring. Inferior products soon give up the ghost.

Check the whippings as well. Some are all show and no guts. Even a 12lb rod imposes a severe burden on the whipping which supports the feet of each rod ring. Tight, neatly aligned threads well impregnated with epoxy or hard varnish are essential. Plain whippings are strong enough on 12, 20 and 30lb tackle. 50 pounders should be underwhipped – that is, the ring feet themselves sit on a layer of thread to prevent side twist. Roller rings are particularly sensitive to side-slip; even 30lb blanks are better underwhipped than left plain. Look *before* you buy.

Line class tackle is fished by the time honoured system of lowering sinker and bait straight down from the hull. Tackle comes to rest either below the boat or drifts downstream. In strong tidal currents there is considerable line belly, which is counteracted by extra sinker weight or wire line. Wire line is thinner than the same breaking strain of nylon monofilament, so the tidal pressure is lower and the tackle stays put without a massive chunk of lead.

In some respects fishing over the gunwales cannot be beaten. Nothing is easier for the beginner. Six or eight anglers work their tackle without tangling their neighbours. Up-and-down tackle control is excellent, both for presenting the bait and fighting a big fish. For the majority of species caught in deepish water you will find no better style of fishing.

A boat anchored in fast-moving water creates a massive 'V' shaped wake that deters some species of fish. That is no problem if the water is deep enough to dissipate the commotion because then fish do swim under the shadow of the hull and find your baited tackle.

In shallow water – less than 35–50ft – the 'V' wake disturbs the seabed to the extent that cautious species of fish like cod, bass and rays move out of the immediate area. Shoals swimming across open ground with the tide divert uptide of the anchor rope to avoid the disturbance.

Nothing in the way of ground baiting or hook bait presentation will prompt them to enter the V of noise and vibration.

The logical answer is to cast baits well away from the boat, so that they lie in quiet water. Sometimes ordinary boat tackle does the trick, but not without a struggle. Short rods and heavy reels are pigs to cast even 50yds. It is a wasted effort anyway because tackle soon drifts out of control in the tide.

Special tackle and methods exist to combat the difficulty of casting and bait anchorage. The style of fishing, known as boatcasting or uptide fishing, is now so well established that it merits equal ranking with conventional fishing. It does not solve all the problems associated with boat fishing and sometimes is quite out of place. But on the right ground in the cod, bass and ray seasons especially, it takes five fish to every one hooked under the hull on conventional gear.

*Long casting over an uptide mark. The technique owes much to
beachcasting, so special long boat rods are essential.*

*Light, sensitive rods that can be held all day make an important
contribution to bigger catches. You miss fewer bites.*

Uptide fishing methods merit a special chapter. For now it is more important to know whether your boat fishing area is one that fishes conventionally or by casting. There is no point your buying a line class boat rod if the waters you fish demand a long cast and special legering techniques. The converse is also true. Ask at the club and watch what happens on the first boat trip. Unless you know beforehand exactly what to buy, borrow club equipment or use the spare tackle normally available on the better charter boats.

Why are uptide rods different?

The pioneers of uptide fishing either extended ordinary boat rods by inserting a longer butt section, or, more commonly, they took along a standard beach casting rod. Finding the beach rod a bit too long and clumsy for boating, they cut down the handle. Eventually, uptide rods evolved as a 9–11ft blank kitted out with standard beach rings and fittings.

Line class specifications are dropped in favour of casting weight classifications. All kinds of uptide rods are available in kit form and ready-built, and the vast majority fall into either the 4oz or 6oz casting weight range. You need two basic rods to cover the full year's fishing, which will be for bass and rays in spring and summer, for cod and whiting in winter. Summer tides and calm seas allow considerable leeway in sinker weight and rod power. Some anglers go down to 1oz sinkers on carp rods. Most standardise on the 4oz rod, which is usually capable of handling between 2 and 5oz.

Heavier tackle is necessary in winter not so much because of the size and power of the fish – though of course a 20lb cod is quite a handful – but because the water is

rougher and the tides much more powerful. 6oz is about right for general uptide casting, yet the rod still needs enough backbone to lob out 8oz on the big spring tides.

The first rod you buy should be chosen according to season and species. Only the local anglers and skippers can put you right on that score. Then it is a matter of finding a suitable rod in the tackle shop – and that is where you could run into trouble. In some areas of the country uptide fishing is in its infancy. If you want a rod, buy a blank and build it yourself or use the mail order service offered by specialist tackle shops which advertise in fishing magazines. Complete rods and kits to make your own are readily available.

General features of uptide rods

The average length is about 9.5ft. Fibreglass blanks are very popular, and conform to the fast-taper design which casts smoothly and powerfully with the short flick necessary from a crowded boat. Most rods comprise a tip section about 6ft long spigot-jointed to a butt of plain fibreglass or with a section of aluminium alloy tube between real seat and butt cap. Check that the spigot seats deeply into the tip and that the joint is well reinforced with whipping threads. Uptide rod spigots take a beating and risk splitting the blank under full load. Some of the more conscientious rod builders add a band of brass to the base of the female joint as extra insurance. It probably is unnecessary, but certainly does no harm.

Reel seats, handle grips and rings are exactly the same as those fitted to beach casting rods. Choose Fuji-type, Seymo or Dynaflo rings in preference to plain wire. The FPS reel seat is far tougher than a

Newell 229 F Multiplier. A robust, precision-made reel for uptide casting and 12–20lb general boat fishing.

snap-lock or a pair of hose clips. Where weight of rod does not bother you, aim for the chromed brass winch fitting. You can depend on it for long service life on the heavier casting rods which toss 6–8oz leads.

Specialist rods

Spinning, trolling and game-fishing rods are sold to a limited number of sea anglers who expand their horizons beyond ordinary boat fishing and uptide casting. In time you may develop an interest of your own, but at the moment it is better to steer clear of anything out of the ordinary, particularly if it means shelling out unnecessary cash. Worse, you may be persuaded to buy specialist tackle to use for standard techniques.

BOAT FISHING REELS

Conventional line class boat reels are different from shore casting and uptide reels. You cannot necessarily use the same reel for all styles of fishing, so it is important to match the rod to the reel *before* you buy. It is so easy to make a serious mistake

The spool pinion gear is the weakest part of a Multiplier's mechanism. High quality metal and engineering ensure long, reliable service.

A pair of classic reels: Penn Senator 113 HL for deep water fishing, and the Magnetic 970, an excellent choice for uptide and general light work.

which completely imbalances the outfit and reduces the chances of good sport.

There are two kinds of reels to consider. The old-style CENTRE PIN reel consists of a frame, axle and large diameter line drum which is turned by finger pressure on two stub handles at its rim. Some reels have built-in brakes which feed line to a running fish; most are controlled by hand pressure on the rim. Their only advantages are speed and power. No geared reel is anywhere near so fast and crane-like as a big centre pin.

The spool of a MULTIPLIER reel sits inside a strong frame mounted on top of the rod. The large winding handle drives the spool through a multiplying gear train. One turn of the handle rotates the spool 2.5–5 times according to the design and size of the reel. Generally, the bigger reels are lower geared to retain plenty of winching power.

At the base of the handle lies a star wheel which controls the brake system. Preset the star wheel so that the spool slips well before line tension rises close to breaking point. Minor adjustments of the wheel help you control heavy fish. Instant fingertip control with no risk of burns and skinned knuckles make the multiplier far easier to use than a centre pin and, as a result, far more popular with modern anglers. Unless you have strong objections choose a multiplier for your first boat reel.

Multipliers are available in a variety of sizes, specifications and prices. The key features of an all-round model which should never be compromised are:

SUGGESTED REELS FOR LINE CLASS RODS

LINE CLASS	POPULAR REELS
12lb	PENN Magpower 970, Squidder 146, Surfmaster 100L
	ABU 6500CA, 7000C, 8000C, ABU12
	MITCHELL 602
	NEWELL 220F
20lb	PENN Senator, Jigmaster, Squidder 146 Magpower 980, Surfmaster 150L, 200L
	ABU 7000C, 8000C, 9000C
	MITCHELL 600
	NEWELL 229F, 235F
30lb	PENN Senator, Magpower 990, Long Beach Squidder 146L, Jigmaster 500, Mariner
	ABU 9000C, 10000C
	MITCHELL 624
	NEWELL 338M
50lb	PENN Senator range, International series Super Mariner

1　Strong spool, preferably of one-piece machined aluminium alloy, brass or bronze.

2　Powerful, smooth drag system with a wide operational range.

3　Tough, saltwater resistant frame and sideplates.

4　Machine cut gears with a ratio high enough to permit rapid handling.

5　Full service and spares back-up by the manufacturer.

How to pick the right model

See which reels your club mates own. As a general recommendation, buy the *smallest* reel compatible with your kind of fishing and which matches the power of your rod. It often pays to stick to the well-known, reputable manufacturers like Penn, Abu, Mitchell and Newell.

Reels for uptide fishing

Reels for uptide fishing have more in keeping with beachcasting. Leading anglers use Penn 970 and 980s, Newell 220F and 229F, or ABU 6500, 7000, 8000C and 9000C. All have casting controls to reduce backlash, high-speed gears, and spools light enough to cast small sinkers a long way. Generally speaking, Japanese reels have lost ground in this market because their gears are too fragile to take prolonged punishment from big fish and strong tides. Top quality

Swedish and American reels are well worth the higher initial investment.

There are very few good uptide reels available beyond the models listed, and basically your choice falls into size – with its direct relationship to the line breaking strain and capacity you prefer – and manufacturer's label. On the whole there is little to choose between most good brands. One point worth considering is versatility. You will see from the preceding list of line class reels that Penn 970 and 980, Newell 220F and 229F, and the larger ABUs appear there as well. This means you can buy one reel to handle both kinds of fishing and save lots of cash.

BASIC MAINTENANCE

Saltwater, sand and grit are the enemy of fine tackle. Without routine maintenance, rods and reels do not last five minutes. Just a little work after every fishing trip cleans off the muck, relubricates reels and allows a close check over whippings, fittings and joints.

Wash off salt and sand in warm water. Unless you dropped the reel into the water

Replace worn whipping and broken rings before you lose that fish of a lifetime.

Regular maintenance saves money. This Abu uptide reel is over 15 years old and still works perfectly.

or on to sand, do not bother about washing the insides every trip. The important step with reels is to wash exterior muck off under a steady stream of water. Ease stubborn grit away with an old toothbrush. Never squirt the reel with a fierce jet of water that forces muck inside.

Rods need the same treatment. Check winch fittings, rings and whippings. A coating of WD40 spray protects bare metal and lubricates the threads of the reel seat without leaving a sticky mess. Spigots should be lightly waxed with candle grease, but brass ferrules are best left clean and *unlubricated*.

Reel lubrication should be carried out sparingly. One drop of oil or grease in the right place is more effective than a gallon slopped inside the frame. All reputable reel manufacturers supply an exploded diagram and parts list for the reel, and include comprehensive maintenance instructions.

3 Lines and accessories

LINES FOR BOAT FISHING

Fishing line is the only link between you and the terminal rig. No matter how good your rod and reel, how fresh the bait and how sharp the hooks, line itself holds the final key to success. Far too many fish are lost through bad lines and poor knots, and there is no excuse for it.

Many anglers spend over £100 on a rod and reel then select the cheapest line in the shop. At the time it seems a good idea to save cash – after all, you still must spend money on bait, petrol and boats. Off they go to sea, drop baits into the water and hook a big fish. The line snaps immediately. Later they discover that the breaking strain is only half that stated on the spool.

The line itself cost perhaps £1 to fill the reel, but the true cost in money alone should take into account the tackle and the extras, all wasted because of that rotten nylon monofilament. Besides that, they lose a big fish and ruined a whole day's sport. Is it worth the risk?

Which line is best?

Monofilament line stretches under pressure by anything up to 25 per cent of its original length. Line stretch imparts a rubbery feel to the tackle when you haul on a big fish. In deep water boat fishing you stand a small risk of losing control of fish that dive for cover or, like conger eels, wriggle into the rocks and weeds. Braided line (also called Dacron) stretches far less and thus offers a margin of insurance.

In extreme circumstances monofilament line may reduce bite sensitivity. Dacron is better in this respect as well, again because it stretches so little under load. The direct feel also makes jigging an artificial lure slightly easier. All told, Dacron does have worthwhile advantages; but they have to be paid for, and despite them Dacron still is losing out to monofilament.

Dacron is more expensive than even the best monofilament lines. It is relatively harder to tie: few knots other than the Jambed Hangman's and Policansky knots work. Braided material is highly susceptible to abrasion and friction burns, and offers little insurance against sudden impact (because it does not stretch). Many anglers find these potential benefits marginal, or even irrelevant to their style of fishing.

Monofilament lines

Monofilament lines – also known collectively as nylon – are manufactured in a wide range of breaking strains, diameters, prices and quality. Nylon is a widely used plastic from which many fishing lines are extruded, but there are other plastics

Du Pont 'Stren' is a best seller worldwide because it offers an excellent blend of diameter, strength, toughness and good knot strength.

equally good if not better.

Regardless of the exact plastics chemistry (which is outside the realms of angling) most monofilament lines offer real advantages to boat men. Not least is the vast selection of lines on sale: you can find a breaking strain, diameter, colour, stretch and flexibility of monofilament that exactly matches your needs. To some extent you can also opt for cheap, medium or expensive brands according to your purse; but as already discussed, that can be false economy.

How do you choose a brand of monofilament?

As a rough guide, look for a modestly stretchy line with a realistic balance between diameter and breaking strain, smooth knotting and good flexibility. The selected breaking strain should be the *minimum* safe for your style of fishing. It is better to err on the light side because such lines cast better and are more controllable.

Breaking strain

It is easy to select a breaking strain for line class boat rods and reels. Stay within ten per cent of the rod's line class figure for safe and efficient angling with little risk of either straining the tackle or prematurely snapping the line.

Should you ever catch a monster fish, the line class of the tackle may be taken into consideration. For acceptance as an

I.G.F.A. line class record, a fish must be landed on line that measures up to the Association's specifications. It is no good submitting 30lb breaking strain line if you want to claim a 20lb line record. The *Line* is what counts, not the rod and reel. Keen I.G.F.A. anglers select their lines very carefully.

You can go wrong by measuring the breaking strain of dry line, or by choosing a brand which the manufacturer has tested dry. All monofilament lines lose strength when saturated. The loss averages 10–15 per cent though some lines are a lot worse than that. Even if you have no interest in the record books, do test line for wet strength. Some that withstand 15lb strain when dry snap at 10lb after long immersion in the sea. Water absorption is a major factor in light tackle angling, so check before you lose that big fish. Soak a few yards of line overnight in water, then test it with a spring balance.

Breaking strain/diameter

Monofilament line of any given breaking strain can be found in a variety of diameters. For example, between 0.30 and

Even small fish abrade line with their sharp teeth. Only high specification nylon has the correct surface resistance.

0.40mm in the case of 15lb test. Thin lines usually cost more, cast farther and pick up less tide pull but may lack shock strength and might even be too stiff. 'Ordinary' grade lines are a little thicker for their breaking strain, but are soft and stretchy – to some extent easier to handle though less precise and sensitive. Choose which ratio you prefer as long as the other qualities of the line suit your fishing. To start with, aim for a middle course.

Some lines lose strength no matter how well you select and tie the knots. Others burn with friction as the coils tighten. Sometimes knot coils dig into the main strand of line and weaken it. All good brands are excellent for knotting – one more good reason to choose them in the first place. Do remember that no monofilament fishing line safely accepts any knot other than those specially designed for it. Blood knot. Palomar, Uni-knot, stand-off loop and leader knot are all indispensable for sea angling.

Which brands are popular?

Sylcast is an all-round monofilament. The modest price balances nicely to the per-

Loading line – 1. Secure the monofilament to the spool with a timber hitch or uni knot.

Loading line – 2. Fill the spool evenly to within 1/8–1/4in of the rim. Maintain moderate tension throughout.

formance; and though it is far from the best line on the market, it is still worth using for non-specialist fishing and for learning. Of the premium quality lines, Maxima, Bayer, Berkley Trilene and Du Pont Stren are firmly established on an international level. Prices? From around £7.50 for 1000yds or 15lb Sylcast to £3.50 for 100yds of 50lb Stren or Trilene. There are hundreds of other brands: try a small spool before investing in large quantities. You may well be disappointed!

Wire lines

Wire line is a useful option to Dacron and monofilament for deep water fishing in very fast tides. It is very slim for its di-ameter, which means that a 30lb wire line will hold bottom with only 8oz of lead in a current severe enough to swill 2lb of lead downstream on ordinary 30lb monofila-ment or Dacron.

Wire stretches even less than braided line, so you need a few yards of monofila-ment inserted between wire and trace to buffer the tackle from impact. Wire tears the insides out of ordinary steel rod rings. Either aluminium oxide lined rings or rollers are a necessity. A tip roller is a must.

Bite sensitivity is enhanced – it is far better than with any stretchy line. Wire is not too hard to handle if you use a narrow but large diameter multiplier like the Penn Mariner, but do be careful of cutting yourself on tightly stretched wire and against the sharp edges of splices in the line.

Loading line on to the reel

First mount your reel on the rod because it is so much easier to work this way. Now tie the end of the line to the core of the spool. A timber hitch or Uni-knot is fine for Dacron and monofilament; wire should be hitched on and twisted around itself for security. Make sure all knots and hitches are snug against the spool core, neatly tied and trimmed.

Load reels evenly and under moderate pressure. Guide the line between finger and thumb. Fill to within 1/4–1/2in of the spool rim according to size of spool and line breaking strain. Experience will suggest the best level for a reel, but, if in doubt, underload rather than overfill.

TACKLE ACCESSORIES

Rod, reel and line are the foundation of your sea fishing tackle. Only a few bits and pieces are necessary to complete the basic outfit, though, of course, you will need waterproof clothing and a tackle box as well. For the moment, pay attention to the essentials, buy the best you can afford and learn to put everything together so that the outfit works well, presents baits perfectly and stays in one piece when a big fish grabs the hook. Hooks, by the way, are discussed within other chapters.

Swivels

Swivels provide a rotating link between main line and trace. In theory a swivel prevents line twist, but its major function is to provide a tough metal anchorage for knots in the main and trace. Lines tend to cut into each other if tied direct. Swivels themselves take a beating, so it pays to buy the best.

Brass and steel swivels are available in a range of sizes. The measuring system for swivels is as obscure as that for hooks, and no two manufacturers agree on the figures anyway. So it is easier to buy according to stated breaking strain or simply by length. Swivels 1/2–3/4in long overall are fine for general boat work. 3/4–1in swivels suit the heavier grades of tackle. The rule is to buy the next bigger size if you are unsure which is correct.

Shark, big conger and skate anglers must use the finest big-game swivels which feature ball-races and sealed barrels. Any kind of good quality swivel is satisfactory for general boat work provided it is strong and corrosion resistant.

Best buys: Berkley and Dexter are the cream of general purpose swivels. Be on your guard for cheap Far Eastern copies that corrode and snap after a few hours in the sea. This is a real and increasing hazard.

Link swivels

Swivels are available with a spring clip on one end for sinker and trace attachment. If the rest of the swivel is strong and the clip itself is well tempered and secure, fine. If not, be very careful indeed. Inferior link swivels open up in mid-cast with frightening results.

Split rings

Hard-chromed steel split rings between 3/8 and 5/8in long, either oval or round, are an

excellent alternative to swivels and probably excel except as an anti-twist device.
If you cannot buy good swivels, or do not
want to pay their high cost, choose split
rings instead. Thousands of anglers now
use them routinely and never regret making the switch. Mustad and Breakaway
Tackle make the best.

Sinkers

A selection of lead weights is essential to
handle varying depths of water and tidal
force. Boat anglers need bomb or conical
weights between 1oz and 2lb according to
the line class of their rig and the water
conditions. Bait size also plays a part: bigger baits inevitably require a few extra

*The emergency kit: pliers, spanners
and screwdriver – the versatile Manley
pliers (top) are standard issue.*

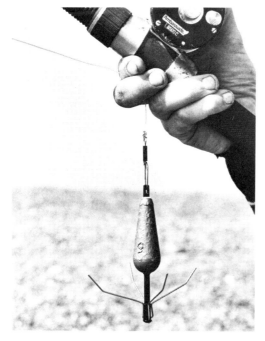

*The new breakaway sinker with
swivelling anchor wires is the perfect
choice for uptide casting and light
bottom fishing.*

ounces of lead to sink and anchor them to
the seabed.

3–6oz boat leads suit most 20lb class
fishing. 30lb tackle is better balanced to 6,
8 and 10oz of lead, but far more may be
required on spring tides. At a stretch, a
30lb rod will handle close to a pound of
lead. 50lb tackle can manage more or less
any size you care to attach, but of course it
is no fun fishing with massive sinkers.
When more than 12oz are required, think
about changing to wire line which allows
an almost 50 per cent drop in sinker weight
without losing bait anchorage. Either buy
sinkers or invest in a multi-weight mould
like the DCA Aquacone and make your
own. Uptide fishermen use standard beach
sinkers, shop bought or poured at home
from DCA Beachbomb or Aquazoom
moulds.

Booms

Booms, spreaders and the general para-
phernalia of trace making used by genera-
tions of sea anglers are obsolescent for
routine bait fishing. Most fancy Christmas
tree brass paternosters and booms have
disappeared already. Perhaps the only successful booms are those used to support a
boat fishing sinker at the base of a running
leger: the idea is for the main line to slide
through the boom so that a biting fish feels
no resistance from the sinker. Clements
and Kilmore booms and their modern plastic equivalents are still widely used because they offer a neat solution to trace
construction. However, an increasing
number of anglers now use a simple link
swivel which is cheaper and usually works
equally well. Flying collar rigs require special wirework which is discussed under
wreck and reef fishing.

Oil, screwdriver and multi-spanner

You can guarantee that if a reel breaks
down, it will do so miles from home. Oil
and screwdriver are absolutely essential,

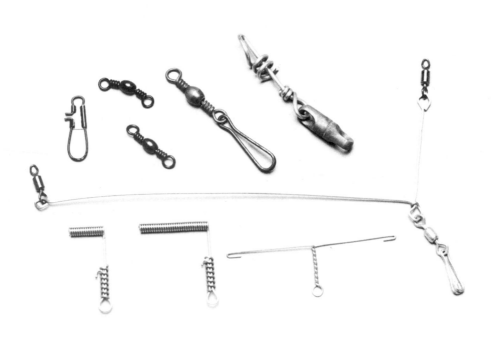

Top line: swivels and clips
Middle: flying collar rig
Bottom: sliding booms and wire paternoster.

*Norwegian swivel with detachable end loop for quick trace changing.
Relatively new on the British market, it is a big advance on traditional swivels.*

and you may want to carry a multi-spanner or adjustable wrench as well. The gadget supplied by the reel maker is quite satisfactory. Store them in a sealed plastic bag, along with spare drag washers and brake blocks. You never know when you will need them in a hurry.

Trace wire

A few feet of 50 and 100lb breaking strain trace wire are a useful standby when you encounter big predatory fish that chomp through nylon. Use it routinely where tope, ling, conger and skate are likely to snatch a bait.

Cable-laid wire with or without an outer shell of transparent nylon is best. Thin wire can be tied to hooks and traces, but 100lb wire certainly requires the special crimp ferrules supplied. Do not buy too much wire at once. Though of stainless steel, it may well tarnish or even rust. Most grades of high-tensile stainless steel are far from immune to corrosion. The stiffer the wire, the more likely it is to deteriorate.

Fishing knives

You will get nowhere without a sharp, reliable knife to cut baits, gut fish, and trim lines. 3–5in single-edged fixed blades are excellent. If you prefer a folding knife, insist that it locks open otherwise there is a good chance it will snap shut on your finger. Keep the blade well honed and oiled. There are stainless steel knives that

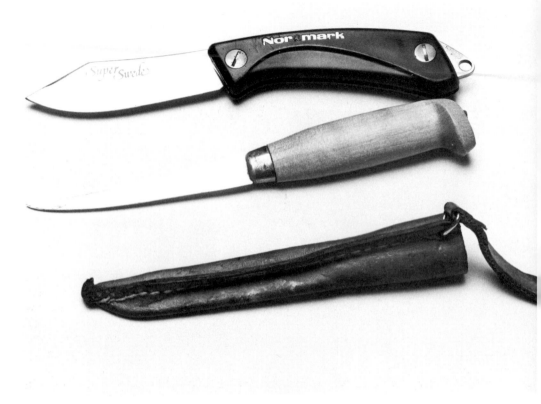

Sharp, rust proof blades are the main feature of good fishing knives. Never use a folding knife that does not lock open.

do not rust, but ordinary high-carbon steel blades sharpen better and retain their edge longer. The trouble is that they soon rust unless washed and oiled after every trip.

Pliers

High-quality long nosed pliers are worth their weight in gold. Use them to cut wire and tough monofilament, unhook fish and to nip wire ferrules and sinker clips. Used with care, pliers are a makeshift spanner to tighten loose screws on reels, mend lures and to reform wire rod rings crushed in transit. Clean and oil them after every trip.

4 Sea fishes and how they feed

BOAT FISHING'S SIX MOST POPULAR SPECIES OF FISH

Literally dozens of species are hauled over the side of boats, some regularly, most only when the skipper has sailed to some specific ground like wrecks and reefs. Important as they are to the sport's kaleidoscope of opportunities ready and waiting for you, tope, turbot, sharks and even conger eels figure only rarely in your catch unless you become a committed wrecker or specialist.

British sea angling relies on about six species to provide all-round and seasonal opportunities from the boat, and it is no bad thing to learn something of their background even before you first toss a bait over the side.

Cod

Hefty cod are a great challenge for boat fishermen. They are powerful fish, easily caught on sporting tackle and, in good seasons at least, hundreds strong on almost every inch of the coastline. Without cod, sea fishing would nosedive into oblivion.

Closely related to pollack, coalfish and haddock, cod are essentially a cold water species distributed from the North Polar region to well south of the English Channel. There are many races of cod, some resident, most migratory. The cod we catch are of the species *Gadus morrhua*, a fast-growing fish that moves into British waters in late October and stays to feed until early April.

The vast majority of cod are migrants, caught only in season. In the colder waters of the far north of our islands and way offshore in very deep water everywhere, cod are resident throughout the year. However, summer sport is always patchy and, with the exception of deep water wrecking, seldom rivals the sheer volume of cod hooked from late autumn onwards. So great is the seasonal effect in many regions that some keen cod anglers do not fish at all during the summer. For them cod is the only species worth hooking.

Cod are primarily an offshore species. Boat anglers always catch most fish because they can get out to the migratory lanes. And they are essentially bottom-feeders which hoover the seabed for anything remotely like food. Their habitat ranges from muddy, fast-running estuaries to offshore wrecks and reefs in clean Atlantic water.

Medium-weight cod are probably the most prized species generally available to British anglers, they are certainly the best to eat.

Bass

Cod are important because they form a high proportion of the sea angler's catch. Bass are far scarcer, smaller and more localised, but still they rank alongside cod on boat fishing's league table. Fanatics – and there are plenty – consider bass to be the ultimate prize on rod and line.

Bass are certainly a handsome fish. Silver, streamlined body and powerful tail are broadly reminiscent of salmon and sea trout; and what bass lack in weight is amply compensated by speed and strength. Few fish venture closer into shallow water or hit baits so hard. Shoals of bass feeding on sandeels and whitebait snatch a lure as fast as you can rebait and cast again.

Above all, bass are fish of wild waters and open coastline. Some of the best marks are spectacular Atlantic sandy bays and rocky inlets backed by mountains and hills. Peak seasons are spring and autumn. Species, season and environment are a formidable emotive combination which for many anglers totally outclasses any other kind of sea fishing.

Bass are migratory in a limited sense. Nobody knows exactly where they go in the colder months, but it is thought they move out to warmer, deeper offshore holes and channels rather than make a full-scale exodus. They do prefer warmer water, so by the very nature of the British Isles that restricts them to the south. Most authorities agree that a line drawn between the Humber and Solent divides our major bass grounds from the barren north. Yet some bass do stray outside their range. And the converse also applies: even in the south there are miles of offshore seabed that produce no bass from one decade to the next.

Boat and shore anglers catch bass. Bass from a boat are in many respects easier to catch because you can home in on shoals feeding around reefs and over sandbanks swept by hard tides. Sandeels, worms, squid and fishbaits drifted downstream, legered or trolled behind a boat take massive numbers of bass from reefs like the Eddystone.

Whiting

Millions of whiting carpet the seabed from late September until Christmas. Shoals are so vast and so easy to catch that nobody who fishes in the sea can possibly fail to connect. Whiting fishing at its peak outstrips the rest of sea fishing combined. Catches of up to a hundred for each angler aboard are common.

Sheer numbers of whiting override any criticism of their sporting merit. On very light tackle they fight hard enough, but any fish that weighs less than 2lb is hardly in the King Kong class. No, it is the certainty and ease of whiting fishing that counts. No fish provides a beginner with such a mighty boost in confidence – on your first trip to sea you could easily land twenty prime fish. There can be no better introduction to the sport; it certainly beats waiting six months for your first bass.

Whiting are migratory fish which move into range of charter boats in early autumn. Like cod, there are two main groups of whiting: migrants and resident fish. Some static shoals move well offshore in summer but still lie within cruising range, and they tend to be much bigger fish than the average run of migratory whiting. English Channel marks and deep-water wrecks and reefs annually produce a small crop of massive whiting over 3lb, but few people fish for them deliberately. They are a bonus which goes with a bag of cod, pollack and congers.

Migrants are never so choosy about location and water depth. Shoals are continuously on the move, chasing small fish, shrimps, and crustaceans along the seabed. Like cod they prefer to feed on the seabed or close by. However, they certainly will move into the upper layers for sandeels and brit.

Dabs and Flounders

Dabs and flounders live all around the British coastline. Flounders are heavier and more prolific; dabs are livelier on the hook and sweeter to eat. Quality and quantity are nicely balanced, so it is hard to say which fish is the more popular. Between them, they account for the vast majority of flatfish hooked from boats. Plaice, turbot and soles are far more exotic but, on the whole, they are a more unpredictable prize for most sea anglers.

Dabs move in and out with season and water temperature. Flounders stay close inshore except during the winter–early spring breeding period. Though tolerant of salinity changes in adult life, flounders are highly sensitive to water conditions in their egg and larval stages. Spawning takes place far out to sea where the water is unaffected by freshwater pouring into the sea from estuaries. Dabs, on the other hand, never care for brackish water. While adult flounders venture into the headwaters of most estuaries, and are occasionally hooked by freshwater anglers, dabs prefer the open sea.

Unlike plaice which thrive in very deep water, dabs are most commonly hooked in less than 100ft; and flounders are perfectly content with just a few feet – or even inches – of water over their backs. As a result, thousands are caught from inshore dinghies working harbour and similar sheltered marks.

The high spot of the dab season is be-

tween late autumn and spring. At the same time the annual seaward run of flounders reaches its peak. Heavy bags are taken from estuaries, in offshore channels and on the edges of sandbanks miles from land. Although both fish are active at the same time, you do not usually catch a really good mixed bag.

Beginners find it hard to tell flounders from dabs. The cynical answer is to taste them. Actually, if you study each fish and compare skin, lateral line and head, you can tell them apart easily enough. Flounders feel smooth if stroked from tail to

With its highly developed olfactory system, plus excellent eyesight, the whiting can locate its food from long range. Greed is its downfall.

head. Dabs are rough. The dab's lateral line is steeply arched around the pelvic fin. The flounder's runs relatively straight. Adult flounders sport a patch of raised lumps on the back of the head and down the lateral line. Both fish grow a spike near the vent but the flounder's is much more pronounced, quite capable of spearing you. Because they prefer sandy bottoms, dabs are usually much lighter skinned. A flounder's natural camouflage is drab and 'dirty'. They even smell stale, while dabs are sweet or odourless.

Thornback rays

Thornback rays are flat-bodied fish, but they are not true flatfish like dabs and flounders. Rays – and skates – are one of the oldest fishes in the sea. They have no bony skeleton; rather, like sharks and dogfish to which they are related, their bodies are toughened by a frame of cartilage. This whole group of fishes is perfectly adapted for its role in the undersea world. Sharks are pelagic killing machines. Rays prefer to hunt on the seabed.

There are many species of ray in British waters. Only the thornback is netted on a large scale for the commercial market. It is the fishmonger's 'skate'. Anglers are keen on the species because it is tasty and also a reasonably challenging fish to catch. Sizes vary considerably. Small male fish weigh less than 5lb, big females run closer to 20lb.

Most areas hold good stocks of thornbacks. The problem is that within any given area just a few hotspots attract the vast majority of fish. That is a great advantage if you know where to drop a bait, but also makes the thornback an easy target for trawlers. A shoal of rays moves in one day; 48 hours later all but a handful of stragglers are frying in batter. Commer-

cially valuable, thornbacks stand little chance of growing old.

Inshore marks produce most thornbacks. In season – late March until September for most areas – groups of rays move in from deep water to hunt rough ground and sandbank edges, often in less than 20ft of water. Over shallows, uptide casting easily outstrips conventional legering. In deeper water you can catch them perfectly well with ordinary boat tackle dropped straight down from the hull.

Thornbacks are good to eat only if correctly prepared. All cartilaginous fish bleed profusely after death, and unless the blood is let out it runs into the meat. Gut the fish, then run the knife blade through the gills and down the side of the backbone where major blood vessels lie. Wash the fish in seawater and store it overnight on ice. Then peel the skin from both sides of the wings. The 'eyeballs' – actually part of the jaw structure – make fine eating as well; and if you are skilled with a filleting knife, try slicing extra strips of meat from the sides of the backbone.

HOW FISH FEED

Saltwater fish are precisely adapted to their environment. Every species has evolved its own special feeding habits linked to migratory route, seasons and to physical strengths and weaknesses of the fish itself. Sharks and tope shadow mackerel shoals along their migratory paths. Conger eels lie in wait for their prey. Soles root through the seabed for shrimps, crabs and worms. Mullet feed on the surface and wrasse lurk in the safety of deep-water rocks and weeds.

Feeding habits are the weakness that anglers exploit. Terminal rigs are designed and baits chosen to fool a fish into

thinking that your worm or strip of fish-bait is either no different from its everyday diet, or, better still, is far more interesting and tasty.

You must choose exactly where to present the tackle: surface, mid-water or on the bottom. The bait should either look attractive, exude the right scent, or vibrate at a frequency that encourages fish to attack. Sometimes just one of those factors is necessary; some fish prefer a combination of two or three.

Underwater visibility in British seas ranges from moderate to nil. Even Atlantic Ocean water is relatively dirty by the time it has swept across the continental shelf and on to the shore. The North Sea is fairly clean well offshore, opaque closer to land. Pollution contributes its share to water opacity but most cloudiness is suspended silt naturally drained into the seas from estuaries and the land or stirred from the seabed by tides and waves.

It is impossible to assess just how well fish can see in cloudy water, or at night for that matter. There is a suggestion that some species have an ability to recognise colours in pitch darkness or in water so deep that colour vision as we know it is distorted. Deep water cuts off the red portion of the spectrum, so human eyes see red as black. Yet fish sometimes hit either a black or red lure but not both. Species such as pollack are choosy even at midnight in quite dirty water.

Shape, colour and size of baits are therefore important. A few fish rely on keen vision to locate their prey at long range. Most use their eyes to guide the final stage of an attack, having reached the general area by scent and vibration. The remark-able numbers of whiting and codling hooked in the eye or around the cheeks may suggest that if necessary a fish will press its eye to the bait to compensate for poor visibility.

Species of fish found in British waters respond far better to the smell, taste and vibration of bait than to the way it looks. Oils and blood exude from most of the natural baits we use. Mackerel, herrings, worms and squid throw off a particularly attractive trail that fish can detect from long distances.

Peeler crabs, sandeels and live baits in general still taste and smell attractive though the flesh is uncut. They produce a natural scent trail, perhaps to attract members of the opposite sex during the breeding season. Hormones, roe and body secretions are easily detectable by predatory fish whose taste buds and olfactory system are highly attuned to scents diluted even millions to one in seawater. Senses of taste and smell are exceedingly well developed in fish that normally live and feed in dirty water.

Vibration plays a varying role in successful fishing. Actively swimming predators such as mackerel, pollack and shoaling bass feed mainly by sight and vibration. When these predators attack shoals of whitebait and sandeels, the blood and oils released into the water act more as a stimulant than a homing device. Predators are drawn to the immediate area from long distances by the scent, then rely on their lateral lines and eyes to pick out an individual target within the shoal of bait.

Any disturbance in water generates a radiating band of vibrations. Some we would hear or feel; others we miss because

(Opposite) A close runner-up to cod in the popularity stakes, thornback rays are number one target for spring and summer inshore fishing.

Understanding of your quarry's lifestyle is an essential foundation of angling technique. If you are fishing for conger eels, the best bait is fresh meat anchored close to the seabed.

our senses operate over too limited a range of frequencies. Fish have ears, too, and they also possess a lateral line running down the flanks. Inside the lateral line is a highly developed sensory system that picks up and interprets a huge spectrum of underwater echoes, 'noises' and vibrations in general. Think of the lateral line as being a superior kind of radar able to build a picture of the surroundings and to locate food. A fish finds and attacks its prey in dark, cloudy water just as accurately and easily as a radar-equipped ship pinpoints a channel buoy. Where fish are attacking their prey by lateral line guidance, a vibrating bait such as a spinner or pirk may prove far more successful than a strip of fishbait, a squid or bunch of worms.

Where fish feed

Terminal rigs take into account the level at which fish swim and the terrain that attracts them. Ordinary legering will miss fish swimming just below the surface or even in midwater. On the other hand, some fish seldom rise above the seabed to feed and always would be lost on float tackle.

Change of position is of necessity slow for most species. Bottom-dwellers would burst their swim bladders were they to make a sudden dash to the surface to grab their food. Most species must rise very slowly and carefully to avoid literally blowing themselves apart. Only a few species like mackerel and its relatives can afford to change depths at will. They lack swim bladders.

Travellers, hunters and ambushers

Migratory species and most residents of wrecks, reefs, offshore sandbanks and channels are continuously on the move. Round fish such as cod, whiting and bass either swim with the current or turn head into tide and drift over the ground at a more leisurely pace. These fish happen upon their food either by chance or, more probably, by drifting until they pick up a scent trail or interesting vibration pattern. Then they swim towards its source. The baits you use and the terminal rig operation are vitally important, otherwise no fish ever finds the hook.

Rays living on open sand and other clean, featureless seabeds move around far less than the roundfish species. Water flowing over the body disc presses them into the seabed, so there is no vast expenditure of energy; thus food intake is comparatively low. Rays can afford to lie on the seabed and test the water for scent and taste as it passes overhead. They feed by waiting for food to come to them, or, if the scent trail is especially attractive and localised, will move out of hiding to quarter the bottom in search of prey. Thornback rays, highly prized by boat fishermen, are very sensitive to bait placement and freshness. Without the right bait in the right place, you may as well not bother to fish.

Flat fish – plaice, turbot, dabs and flounders – also use their body shape to lay in ambush in the tide. They react to scent, sight and vibration. Flat fish wait until food moves close, or until the tide eases, then sneak along the seabed to grab their prey. Flashing spoons, colourful beads and spinners encourage an attack, hence the development of special rigs for flounders and plaice especially. Moving the bait rather than leaving it at anchor may encourage more bites.

Ambush feeders are drawn towards rocks and weeds where they lie up in crevices, under stones and buried in sandy patches between rough outcrops. They dash out of hiding to grab shrimps, small fish, crabs and any other suitable prey. Conger eels spend much of their time just waiting for something to turn up. Bass, pollack, cod and other species which do not find it profitable to hide up, or are physically unable to blend well enough into the background, tend to creep through weeds and gullies instead. They watch for sandeels and whitebait to drift past close overhead in the clear water above the rocks. Within the restrictions of swim bladder pressure, they might rocket several feet towards the surface. Examine a pollack with its well defined underjaw and big eyes to appreciate how well it is adapted to attacking from below. No wonder pollack rigs are often more productively fished a little above the seabed and moving baits are preferred.

Scavengers and predators

Scavengers eat fresh food, dead creatures and garbage in general. Strict predators kill their own prey. Very few species of fish are totally either scavenger or predator but many have distinct preferences which influence your bait and terminal rig selections. Although bottom fishing with worms and fish strips seems to produce reasonably good results with a variety of fish, there are occasions when a specialised approach hits the jackpot.

Conger eels and rays living along un-spoilt, rugged coastline love fresh meat. Small live pouting and mackerel or big lively sandeels are fine conger baits. Fresh-ly killed fish and absolutely perfect frozen squid also produce the goods. Rays also are very fussy indeed when they want to be. Stale baits of any kind fail because big predators in their natural habitat are used to grabbing live food. Freshly filleted baits work well in most circumstances because the taste and smell are so attractive that the fish pays no heed to lack of vibration and other signs of life.

The same species drawn to harbours and estuaries by easy feeding on offal and rub-bish thrown from fishing boats or fish-processing plants soon learn that it is easier to scavenge than to hunt. Harbour eels and big rays attack less-than-perfect baits, perhaps even in preference to live baits. Any species including normally strict predators can be weaned off their normal diet and away from natural pre-judices if alternatives are easily available.

Cod, whiting, bass and flat fish are mixed feeders, equally content to run down a lively bait or to grub along the seabed for anything remotely edible. Some home in on putrefying flesh. Dabs are par-tial to a helping of stinking lugworms so old you must pour them on to the hook. At the other extreme, whiting are possibly the most fussy fish in the group. It is no surprise if they attack really fresh mack-erel strips but ignore those left out of the freezer for a couple of days.

Grabbers and teasers

Competition for food is fierce. Within a shoal of cod, bass or whiting, only the quick survive. Whether food is alive or dead, cod rush in and suck down a mouth-ful – stones, sand and all. Most species of fish share the same trait, though smaller ones are more precise in the way they attack. Cod are blundering feeders built like mechanical shovels; flatties, whiting and school bass favour a more clinical, incisive attack. Either way, you can bet that most fish will hook themselves on the right terminal rig.

Solitary fish such as congers, big rays of all species and skate have plenty of time to examine a bait. Tope, smoothounds and shoaling thornback rays, haddock and big-ger bass feed with relative caution even though they face some competition. Tim-ing the strike may be a problem for begin-ners. Fish that play with baits rather than grab and swallow in one go may fiddle with the trace for a long time before swal-lowing or ignoring the bait.

Rays have a special problem. Their bulk and anatomy encourage a slow, shuffling engulfment of baits lying on the seabed. During the preliminary stages of their attack, many of these big, naturally cau-tious fish are sensitive to any resistance from line or sinker. Some drop the bait and run. Others take it but halfheartedly. The hook skids out when you strike.

(Opposite) Sharks are the ultimate predator. Porbeagles and blues are the most common British species.

Effects of tide, season and waves

Best fishing times often coincide with the fastest run of tide that occurs midway between high and low water on both ebb and flood. Spring tides encourage fish to feed, and migratory species tend to work along the coast in stages prompted by the faster flow of water. Cod are well known to hang around sandbanks and channels during the neap tides then travel long distances on the springs.

Tides make a real difference to boat fishing prospects and also influence the tackle you use. Spring tides generally require heavy sinkers and streamlined terminal rigs. And while a big tide may activate the species themselves, it may also run so fast and deep that fishing becomes impossible.

Long-range voyages to deep water wrecks and distant sandbanks are absolutely dependent on reasonably settled weather of course. Fish themselves are less affected, but sudden changes in barometric pressure may switch off the bites or even trigger a feeding spree. Cold weather and falling water temperature either stop fish feeding or reduce their appetites. Small baits and light tackle sometimes catch fish when conventional methods fail.

5 Baits for boat fishermen

INTRODUCTION TO BAITS

Successful boat fishermen know that good bait is often the difference between a big catch and mediocre results. Match anglers, in particular, go to any lengths to ensure a supply of premium grade worms, crabs, squid, mackerel or whichever baits are best for the available species of fish.

Mostly, we fish with natural baits dug from the beach, picked up under rocks, caught from the sea by hook or net. Most experienced anglers would prefer to collect and dig their own bait, though it does not always make sense to do so. If you live inland, petrol and wasted time add up to more than the cash price of bait ordered from a professional digger or tackle shop. However, if there is time to root along the seashore, you may end up with better quality bait and a wider selection.

Freshness and choice

Species of fish each have favourite diets. Thornback rays are easier to hook on chunks of mackerel and herring than on a bunch of lugworms. That is not to say they never eat lugworms; but overall you would find worms a poor alternative. Conger eels and tope share the same preferences. Like most big predatory species they feed on generous helpings of meat – whole mackerel, herrings, sandeels and big squid.

It makes no sense for a tope to grub around for 3in lugworms.

Bass, flatfish, codling and whiting are scroungers. They snatch small fish, shrimps and crabs, worms and shellfish. If one particular kind of food is plentiful and easily caught, most species of fish become preoccupied: summer bass in rocky ground usually prefer peeler and soft crabs. Most of the time, though, no bass can afford to be so choosy. Ragworms, lugworms and sandeels work equally well on the hook.

First, then, match your bait to the species and how it normally feeds. Keep an eye on localised and often short-lived preferences. Carry a reasonable selection of baits aimed either at general fishing for anything that turns up, or to tempt one or two species in particular.

THE POPULAR BAITS

Most marine creatures can be used as bait. Usually we rely on a traditional selection that catches all kinds of fish year in, year out. Try more exotic hookbaits if you like, but make it your priority to learn about the standard range. Remember that baits which excel in one area may not catch a single fish 50 miles up the coast. Local knowledge is worth a fortune.

Lugworms

Lugworms are soft reddish-brown worms with fat bodies and long, sand-filled tails. Common around the entire British coastline, they live on beaches with a reasonable depth of sand, mud or muddy grit. Each worm spends most of its life buried in a *U* shaped tube, one end open, the other capped by a tell-tale spiral cast. They form colonies millions strong . . . unless bait diggers get them first.

Lugworms live on the beaches all year round. Colonies are easier to spot in summer when worms grow quickly in preparation for the short breeding season in late autumn. Cold winds and lower water temperature drive them deep into the sand throughout winter and early spring.

Lugworms are dug either individually or by trenching through the colony with a broad tined fork. Store them between layers of newspaper in a wooden box. Some anglers keep their worms in a bucket of water instead, but that is less effective because immersed lugworms usually empty themselves. The muck normally contained in the guts is an important part of the bait and certainly toughens it.

Lugworms are mounted on the trace

Lugworms should be threaded on to a long shanked, fine wire hook.

Ragworm is a most effective summer bait for bass and flatfish.

singly or in bunches. Choose a number of worms appropriate to the size of the fish. Dabs and flounders are happy with a single 1–3 inch worm; four or five big worms crammed on to a hook are a better offering for offshore cod. Experience soon tells you how many worms to use for any particular species. Thread the bait from head to tail along a reasonably long-shanked fine wire hook. Aberdeen and Viking models are useful for worm fishing. The size of hook balances the number of worms threaded on and the size of the fish you hope to catch. Use a range of hooks between size 4 and 8/0 to cover most species from soles to big cod.

Lugworms work best for species of fish that rely on scent and taste to locate their prey. Even two or three exude a powerful slick of blood and juices into the tide. The trail is strong at first, but soon dies off as tide sucks the bait empty. Shrimps and crabs rip lugworms to shreds within minutes. In all, it pays to change your bait regularly, at least every 20 minutes.

Ragworms

Many sea worms qualify for the name ragworm. Those used as baits include king ragworm which may exceed 2ft long, smaller harbour ragworms and the white or silver ragworm, a relatively uncommon species highly prized by match anglers. Compared to the lugworm, ragworms are long and thin, fringed with soft paddles and well armed with a pair of sharp pincers at the head. Most species are red, brown or greenish – exactly the right colour for camouflage. Unlike lugworms which sit in a tunnel and eat vegetable matter, rag-worms are predators that burrow through the seabed or swim freely in search of a meal.

King and harbour ragworms prefer thick mud or a mixture of mud and gravel. Other species live under the stones and weeds of a rocky shoreline. And some like the white ragworm show a preference for sand. In almost every case the best worms are found in waterlogged sections of beach because unlike lugworms they are not too keen on being stranded high and dry at low tide.

Ragworms are dug with a fork. Walk along the seashore near low water mark, and you may see jets of dirty water swirl from the mud and grit. Chances are that a ragworm is at work, so dig through the immediate area until you unearth him. Worms live either alone or more often in small colonies. The whole colony moves along the beach, travelling several yards on a tide when the mood takes them.

Freshly dug king and harbour ragworms are soft and fragile. Store them in a bucket of water until you get home, then wrap them in layers of newspaper in which they dry out, toughen and become even redder. The white ragworm is a much tougher and fiercer worm best stored in cold seawater.

White and king ragworms are used whole or broken into suitable chunks. Fine wire, long-shanked hooks hold bait together and enhance its presentation. Small fish such as flatties, eels and school bass prefer a piece of worm 1–3in long on size 4–1/0 hooks. Big bass and rays are happier with a generous helping: a whole king ragworm threaded on to a 4/0–8/0

Aberdeen hook. Though cod, in general, prefer lugworms to ragworms, they love white rag. Use whole worms (plus lug if necessary to add bulk) on fine wire hooks in the 1/0–4/0 bracket. Whipped shanks are better than eyes or spades because they do not burst the worm when it is pushed on to the hook and threaded up towards the trace.

Herrings and mackerel

Mackerel are never around when you need them. Summer shoals disappear and by late autumn you are left wishing for a dozen fresh fish to fillet for conger and ray baits, or to chop into neat chunks for whit-ing fishing. Good herrings are even more elusive.

Feather or spin for mackerel whenever you have chance, then deep freeze as many as you can for baits. There is no substitute for absolutely fresh bait, but mackerel frozen straight from the sea are a reasonable alternative. Most hungry spe-cies will accept them from the hook, though wily conger and rays never settle for second best.

Vast numbers of mackerel and herrings are netted by the commercial fleets, and they are excellent bait if blast frozen aboard ship or within hours of being landed. Most fish end up on a fishmonger's slab and though perfectly fit for us to eat are far from fresh as far as sea fish are concerned. Thornback rays immediately sniff the difference between a chunk of fresh mackerel and a slice from the High Street.

Buy your fish baits on the quayside or

(Opposite) Mackerel feathering. Great sport in itself, and your best guarantee of the finest bait for predatory species.

from a fish wholesaler. Most dealers insist you buy a minimum quantity, usually a frozen block weighing around a stone. Store the block in a freezer and break off enough for a single fishing trip by smashing the frozen pack on the floor. There is no need to thaw the lot to separate half a dozen fish.

Most fish eat mackerel and herring. Smaller species take slivers of skin and flesh sliced from a fillet. Nick the bend and point of the hook through the skin to leave plenty of meat dangling. If long casts up-tide of the boat are necessary, insert the hook back and forth a few times to package the bait securely. Fine-wire hooks in the size 4–1/0 range are perfect.

Medium size species like thornback rays, big bass, pollack and shore-caught conger eels favour a larger strip, half a fillet, or a 1in cross-sectional chunk complete with backbone and guts. Much of the blood and oils lie in the gut cavity, so it makes little sense to waste it. Fix the bait on to 2/0–8/0 medium weight hooks like Viking and O'Shaughnessy, and be sure to leave the point and bend lying exposed for better striking. If necessary, use a wire trace.

Really big fish – sharks, skate and 40lb-plus tope and conger – usually prefer a whole fish with the hook and trace threaded all the way down from tail to head. The extra advantage of a big bait is that smaller fish either leave it alone or cannot swallow it. The risk, though, is to suppose that all big fish automatically go for the big meal. Sometimes half a herring or a mackerel head and shoulders produce the goods where a whole fish lies un-noticed. Ring the changes if the action is slow. You need tough hooks for big fish.

The ultimate hook for all heavyweight sea angling is a Mustad Seamaster 2/0–10/0.

Squid

Squid are quite common in our waters. Sometimes, you hook them on ordinary sea tackle fished in deep water. Trawlers net them as well, but seldom intentionally. Most of the squid sold in Britain for food and bait arrives from Europe and California. Frozen blocks of squid between 4 and 12in long are freely available through fish shops and the wholesale trade.

In some respects squid is a strange bait. As an all-rounder for boat fishing it is really a non-starter in the race against worms, crabs, sandeels and fish. You could cast squid for months on end without catching one fish.

For some reason, though, a high proportion of specimen bass, rays and other common offshore species fall to legered squid. It is therefore a bait of extremes; an all or nothing attempt to single out a big fish. If you have the patience to fish day in, day out on the off-chance of landing monster bass or cod, squid is a good bait.

Hooks for squid fishing range from fine wire Aberdeens for slivers of meat cut from the main body and sections of tentacle, to Mustad Seamasters for big whole squid legered for congers. Use monofilament or wire traces as appropriate.

Crabs

Common green shore crabs infest most beaches and extend right out to the deeps. Many of the fish you gut will contain at

(Opposite) Thornbacks are highly sensitive to bait freshness. Only absolutely perfect squid is accepted.

least a few crabs; sometimes the belly is stuffed to bursting point. The paradox is that relatively few species of fish ever take a hardbacked crab from the hook. As bait they are worse than useless except for wrasse and the occasional smoothound.

At stages during its life cycle when old shells become too small, crabs shed their armour and grow a new set. The new shell develops as a perfectly coloured but soft skin lying under the old casing. When the shedding process is about to take place, the crab is known as a peeler. If you lift up the back edge of the carapace, you can see the soft new skin beneath. At this stage of

its life and a few days later when the old shell falls off, the crab is very much in demand by anglers, other crabs and most fish in the sea. It is called a softy of softback.

Crabs breed during the peeler and soft stages. To attract other crabs they emit powerful attractors called pheromones. Fish also detect the scent, and are quick to home in for a ready meal. Anglers who know just how effective crab baits are for flounders, dabs, bass, codling, and dozens more beach and shore species are quick on the uptake as well. In season it is hard to find enough softies and peelers to go round.

Mackerel properly cut and filleted for the hook. The head is a good ray and conger bait.

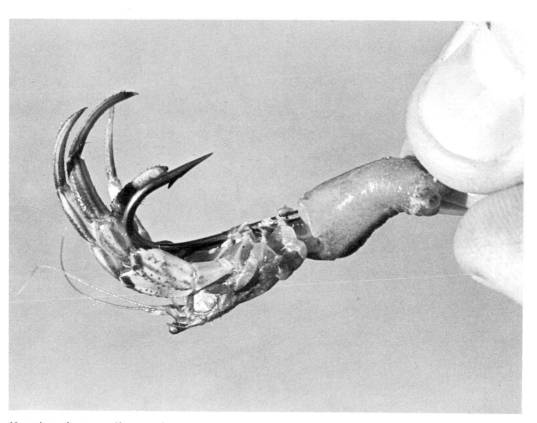

Hermit crabs are easily netted, and make a tempting bait for most species, especially smoothhounds.

Green shore crabs hide under rocks on the foreshore, among weeds and in mud. Scrape them out, turn over stones and root through weed patches. You will find dozens of crabs, and in the warmer months a good proportion are peelers or softies. Store in cool, damp seaweed and fish them whole or in chunks.

Small pieces of crab can be directly impaled on fine wire hooks of a size chosen to suit both bait and species of fish. Whole crabs are a little more tricky to mount up and cast. Softies may be so jelly-like that the hook tears out on a 50yd lob. The answer is to strap the crab to the bend and shank of the hook with layers of shearing elastic or several turns of rubber band.

Edibles and velvet swimmers are super baits for bass, but not quite as good as green crabs for the majority of species. The only crab to rival the green one is the hermit. Dozens can be hauled out in a drop net baited with scraps of fish. As well as being a devastating bait, hermits have the further advantage of always being ready for the hook. The rear end of the creature is always soft.

Sandeels

Anglers on the western coast of England and in Cornwall value sandeels for boat fishing. Fishermen elsewhere have been slow to experiment, yet some who do substitute a packet of frozen eels for their normal lugworms and mackerel are often rewarded with surprisingly good catches of

57

bass, flatties, codling and whiting. In fact, most of the species found along the coasts and offshore sometimes take sandeels from the hook.

Sandeels prefer clear water and reasonably high temperatures. They disappear from the shallows in autumn and will not come back until the seas warm in the May sunshine. Greater and lesser sandeels – also called lance, launce and a dozen more local names – form massive shoals easily trapped by seine nets worked from dinghies and small fishing boats.

If you want fresh, live sandeels, net your own or scrape them from the beach with a special rake that slips around the eel's body and draws it clear of the sand. A bucket of fresh water keeps eels lively for a few hours. Long term storage depends on a well aerated tank kept cool and dark. The easiest way to keep sandeels alive all day is to lay them inside a *dry* insulated box filled with icepacks. Deep frozen, sandeels last for months.

Hook sizes vary according to bait length and species sought. Size 2–6/0 Aberdeens and Vikings are suitable for all-round boat fishing. Bass anglers say that silver or gilt hooks are less conspicuous than bronze. Sometimes it makes a difference for bass fishing in clear water, but for the majority of species hook size and colour amount to very little.

(Opposite) Sandeels would certainly become our premier sea bait were they more widely available. Every species from dabs to shark will eat them, especially if they are fished alive. The baby mullet in the photograph was netted accidentally. Conservationists would return it – but most keen anglers know a good bait when they see one!

6 How to strike and play a fish

Comments under this heading apply to all styles of boat fishing. Many anglers strike ineffectively or at the wrong time. Countless fish are missed altogether, or, at the other extreme, hooked in the guts instead of neatly in the jaws. It could fairly be said that the fundamental mechanics of sinking a hook into the fish's jaws then fighting the beast to the side of the boat are a source of great confusion and embarrassment to beginners, therefore we include this small chapter as a working guide for newcomers who have yet to feel their first bite on a boat rod.

The most common mistakes are striking too soon, striking too softly and failing to follow through. Typically, an angler feels the bite, immediately jerks on the line, then stops and watches the rod tip to see if the fish is hooked. During that second's breathing space his fish sometimes escapes even if it was hooked initially.

Striking and hooking guidelines:

Small roundfish like whiting, pout, bream, haddock, codling and wrasse are fairly quick-biting species. Fast, rattling bites can be hit after a few good knocks appear on the rod tip. Be confident – once you

decide to move, hit the fish firmly.

Flatfish, rays, bull huss and lesser spotted dogs give fairly gentle but persistent bites that must be given plenty of time to develop. They seldom leave a bait, and usually swallow it if you wait too long. Fish destined for the frying pan call for a delayed strike. To return them alive, strike earlier and accept the trade off between missing some fish and avoiding serious wounding.

Large fish like congers and big cod often bite much more gently than their size would suggest, although it is usually possible especially with wire line to feel a substantial weight to the bite. Allow them plenty of time; perhaps give some slack line which sometimes boosts a big fish's confidence enough to trigger a very positive attack.

Bites on the drift from all species tend to be much quicker and more decisive than bites on bottom-fished baits. With moving baits fish have to make up their minds very quickly, and as a result the strike itself is much more prompt than when fishing at anchor.

Striking must take up any belly in the line and, in the case of nylon, also absorb a certain amount of stretch. Sharp bites from small fish should be treated to a full sweep of the rod coupled with a few turns

(Opposite) Safely in the net – keep cool, take your time, and do as the skipper says.

of the reel. Slower bites are better handled by winding down until you feel the fish's weight, then lifting with the rod tip.

Playing a fish calls for maintaining plenty of pressure on the rod. Do not try to skulldrag the beast – such eagerness to see the fish leads to many a needless disaster. Instead, maintain continuous pressure and let the fish run against the drag if it wants. Even if tackle and hookhold are man enough to crank your fish directly to the boat while it is still fresh and kicking, it will be desperately hard to gaff or net.

Pumping is the only real skill you have to learn. You see, it is virtually impossible to hold the rod and simply crank line back on to the reel. Either your wrist grows numb from the strain or the line breaks. And in extreme conditions where the fish is very tough and the line itself is adequately strong, the reel's gears strip or the spool literally explodes out of the sideplates. Pirk fishing, for reasons explained in the relevant chapter, is just about the only situation where it pays to crank the handle.

The practical alternative is to pump line back on the reel. Most of the strain by-passes the reel that way, and fighting a fish is far less demanding on the angler as well. This is what you do. Lift the rod tip against the fish's weight until, within reason, you reach maximum upward extension. Do not crank the reel while you lift. Now, quickly and smoothly drop the rod tip back to the water, again working through a comfortable arc. At the same time – and timing is important if you are to avoid loose coils or line flowing on to the spool – wind in the slack until you feel the fish's weight once more. Stop winding, lift the rod, drop and wind, lift, drop . . . and so on. Keep doing that until the fish is beaten and drifts alongside. Should the fish suddenly dive or run while you are pumping, the reel's drag system – properly adjusted of course – takes care of sudden stress that would otherwise snap the line.

Fish that are too big or too desirable to be simply swung aboard should be netted, gaffed or even grabbed by hand. All this is most simply achieved once the fish is tired and quiescent. Normal approved procedure is for the angler to lead the fish to the waiting implement. In practice, most charter skippers take net to fish as soon as it comes within range . . . usually because they lack faith in the angler!

(Opposite) Drop the rod, wind in the slack line, then lift. That is the secret of pumping a big fish. Remember to pre-set the drag.

7 Bottom fishing

The bulk of British boat fishing is carried out at anchor over sand, mud, shingle, broken rock or combinations of these and in water from 35–150ft deep. Though never producing the massive catches that wreck fishing yields, at best it still offers top quality sport for a very wide range of species.

The skipper chooses marks on his knowledge of the fish sought, season, weather and tides. For turbot he may head for an offshore bank of sand and shingle scoured by fierce tides and currents where the big flatties lie in the lee of the bank to watch and wait for sandeels. For early season spurdogs he might steam miles offshore where the fish shoal in deep water ledges and gullies.

Few bottom fishing skippers really need sophisticated electronic navigation aids like Decca. Generally, they operate reasonably close to shore and locate their marks by cross-bearings or by running a compass course at known speed and time. Having found the right area, they pinpoint the feeding spot with the aid of an echo sounder. However productive a patch of ground may be there are likely to be features on it where fish concentrate – hollows, a small bank, a rocky area. All of them show up on the sounder's graph paper.

To allow for the currents, the boat is taken uptide of the mark before the anchor is dropped. Now, the tide washes the fishing tackle downstream into the target zone, but it might be necessary to re-anchor on the turn of the tide if, say, a specific small gully is being fished.

So there you are: the boat is riding nicely at anchor, the sun shines on a calm sea. What next? There are countless permutations of approach, bait, tackle and tactics. To begin, concentrate on the basic guidelines shown here and you will not go far wrong. Methods that catch whiting will also hammer codling or pouting on different ground. If you catch big winter cod in 20 fathoms of screaming tide you can, with minor adjustments, tackle anything else that lives in such conditions.

A very successful angling career can begin without much understanding of the mechanics or even of fish themselves. Most of the time, those are dictated by which port you sail from, exactly where the skipper decides to anchor, season, tides and migration patterns. You pay the man at the wheel to find fish, then for the most part it is a matter of dropping baits over the gunwale.

However, the keen beginner soon starts to ask questions: why do we use herring baits today, worms tomorrow? Why can't you catch tope on short nylon traces? Why use wire lines to hook winter cod in deep, fast-running tides? In-depth knowledge results from experience, and no book can give you that. Our aim here is to provide an overview of the various species and

(Opposite) On a really hectic day, you will hook whiting like this one by the dozen – sometimes three at once.

techniques that surround bottom fishing from a boat anchored in deep water. Given that inside information, you will feel much more at home if, for example, the skipper says, 'Well lads, the cod are down 120ft and the tide's rising fast . . . so put down a big chunk of squid on wire line'.

WHITING

Whiting swim in large shoals usually over a bottom of sand or light shingle, and are often sought after in modest depths of 40–

80ft and in gentle tides. (They live in deep, fast water as well, but are much less fun to catch because tackle must be unduly heavy.)

A light rod does the job. 20lb class tackle is more than strong enough and many anglers go substantially lighter when conditions allow. The improved bite detection of light rods can even produce a higher catch rate.

Virtually any terminal rig will catch these bold feeders, but for maximum efficiency a short-snooded three hook paternoster armed with fine wire 1/0 or 2/0

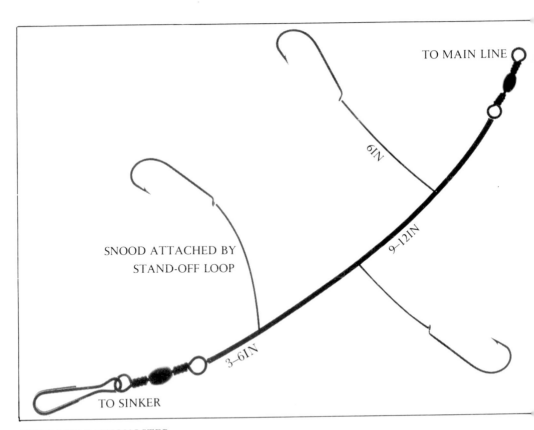

TO MAIN LINE

6IN

9–12IN

SNOOD ATTACHED BY
STAND-OFF LOOP

3–6IN

TO SINKER

THE BASIC PATERNOSTER

Winter cod. Fishing is the high spot of any sea angler's year.

hooks permits a fast and tangle-free return to bottom after each haul. Baited feathers or small plastic squids often enhance catches of this aggressive little predator.

Offshore whiting, especially big ones, are mainly fish eaters. Strips of mackerel and herring around 3 × 1in are a cheap, killing bait. Expensive lugworms are better saved for more choosy species.

Let your paternoster drop quickly through the water, and prevent a backlash by thumbing the rotating spool. When the lead hits bottom, throw the reel in gear, take up slack line and wait. If whiting are around, you should get a bite within minutes; certainly after baits have been down for twenty minutes the scent trail should draw eager fish within range of the boat. A sink-and-draw action sometimes triggers the action when whiting are slow to feed.

Whiting bites are quick and rattling. Do not strike at the first peck. Strike after a few confident pulls on the rod top, or after the tip bangs down and stays there. Strike firmly with a full sweep of the rod, and reel in quickly at the same time. You will feel the whiting jerk and tug. Wind him (or them) smoothly to the surface and into the boat. In the event of a clean miss – and there will be some – drop the gear straight back down. You will often get another bite immediately.

COD

Although we have only one species of cod in Britain, our angling approach must be made according to season and location. Winter cod in relatively shallow areas are

hooked by boatcasting, but where the water gets deep, tides fierce and cod heavy a totally different tactic is required.

Traditional cod fishing methods involve big juicy baits fished hard against the bottom and allowed to drift downstream from the back of the boat. Fish home in to smell, movement and vibration. If the tide is strong – and big cod relish hard currents, feeding through the peak of the run – this means fishing with wire line.

The tackle needed for wire is detailed elsewhere; for the moment, remember that a leader of 6–10ft of 30–50lb monofil is essential for the sinker to run on and to ensure that the tackle stretches enough. The best end rig is a simple running leger with a 5–10ft trace of 30–50lb monofil. The harder the tide the longer the trace you can and should use.

Lugworm and Calamari squid are the two outstanding baits for winter cod. Check local preferences though because they are not necessarily interchangeable over every mark. An uptrace attractor such as a spoon of metal or white plastic, or even a big plastic squid, sometimes improves catches no matter which natural bait is on the hook. 6/0–8/0 hooks are none too big, and the successful trend is to fish two in Pennell fashion.

Wire line demands excellent tackle control. Birdsnests are devastating! Let the tackle down under firm thumb pressure and stop the spool as soon as the sinker touches bottom. Then lift the sinker a couple of feet and let the tide take it downstream. The lead should be heavy enough that it is necessary to let out no more than 4–5yds of line before the tackle bumps again. In this fashion the bait can be worked for 100yds astern, covering lots of ground.

Because wire has no discernible stretch, bites are very obvious even at long range. They are often gentle though; in fact, the bigger the cod, the more softly it attacks. Do not rush the strike. Instead, let the fish pull line from the spool against light thumb pressure until you are confident that the bait has been thoroughly engulfed. Then put the reel in gear, wind up the slack until the rod goes 'heavy', and lift into the strike.

RAYS

Thornback rays are by far the most common species hooked from British boats. With the exception of small-eyed rays and stingrays, other species are relatively uncommon, mostly taken while anglers are fishing for other than the ray family.

The thornback has a very wide distribution, while the painted ray favours a number of specialised hotspots around the south and west coasts. Thornbacks eat virtually anything, with a preference for crustaceans, shellfish and small fish. Painted rays are mainly fish eaters.

Suppose you are fishing in an area where both species overlap. It is April, early in the season for rays, and the boat lies offshore over 100ft of water. As spring wears on both species will creep closer to the shoreline, but this soon after winter they much prefer the warmer water found in greater depths. The bottom is mainly sand with patches of scrubby rock. Tide is modest.

Rays feed primarily by smell and will

(Opposite) Thornback rays two at a time. Male and female are sometimes caught together on the same hook.

Hook a smoothhound in shallow water, and watch out for the fireworks. Let your fish run, or she will smash the line.

sidle up to their prey and pounce on it, pinning the victim under their wings. Then they manoeuvre until the mouth is positioned for some serious eating. The bait must be presented on a 4–6ft flowing trace lying on the bottom. Rays have blunt, flat teeth so wire is unnecessary; 35lb monofilament nylon is completely ray-proof. 4/0–5/0 O'Shaughnessy hooks are perfect for herring and mackerel baits, and sandeels are best presented on a fine wire Spearpoint Boat hook.

Lower the tackle slowly to prevent trace tangling with main line. Trot the bait downstream if there is enough tide running – that way you cover as much ground as possible. Lift the sinker to make the tackle drift, lower it to re-anchor. Bites are usually gentle and should be given plenty of time to develop. Hit a ray too early and you will either hook it in the wing or miss completely. Drive in the hook, then lift the fish. Rays do not put up any fight worth speaking about, though a big thornback kiting against a fierce ebb tide does strain 20lb line to its limits unless the reel's drag is correctly preset.

SMOOTHOUNDS

These fish are becoming an increasingly important part of the angling year as it is realised that they are more widely distributed than previously believed. A smoothie has a mouth and teeth very similar to a ray's, and it enjoys a similar lifestyle with the bulk of its diet being crabs of one sort or another. One major benefit is its willingness to feed even in the dog days of high summer when nothing else stirs.

Tackle and tactics for smoothhounds are identical to those outlined for rays, except that baits should be peeler crab, hermit crab or even hardbacked shore crabs. Ragworm catches some fish but is better restricted to shallow water. No other bait is worth using.

Bites vary widely from gentle knocks to rod bending runs. They should be struck quite early. Smoothhounds fight on the run, not as fast as tope but with tremendous power and determination. Let them take line or they will break you. They have great stamina also – hooked on light tackle a smoothhound gives you a battle to remember.

TURBOT AND BRILL

Both species are widely distributed but they are fished for only in spots where they congregate, usually offshore banks of sand and gravel with a substantial population of sandeels. The fish lie in gutters and behind banks, out of the scouring tide. From those natural ambush points these perfectly camouflaged predators pounce on small fish that venture too close.

The boat is anchored well uptide of the mark and baits are trotted back on an 8–10ft trace of 20–35lb monofilament. Although the tide is very strong, the water is shallow and thus wire is seldom necessary.

Key to success is bait presentation. It should look and move like a live sandeel. A lively sandeel is the finest bait but for some reason a whole dead sandeel is less attractive than a long fillet of eel or even a strip of mackerel. Perhaps the whole fish's backbone kills the natural fluttering action?

Turbot and brill have colossal mouths but hook size must be more in keeping with the bait. Delicate live sandeels struggle to carry more than a 4/0 Aberdeen hook while a whole mackerel fillet will hide a 6/0 O'Shaughnessy.

As with cod fishing, the bait is worked carefully behind the boat, searching the gullies where fish lie. Bites show as a series of firm pulls and it is important to allow some slack line and plenty of time for the bait to be sucked in. If you like, have a cup of coffee before you tighten up and strike. These big flatties are too rare and desirable to lose unnecessarily.

TOPE

This shark-like predator is likely to turn up anywhere when there is an adequate supply of food – and that includes mackerel, herring, sandeels, flatfish or any of the smaller members of the cod family. Tope in deep water give a rather dour fight, whilst in shallows they battle like demons. However, there are few places left where tope are freely available in shallow water. Today most specialist fishing is done in moderate tides, 50–90ft of water and over a sand/shingle bottom.

Tope are running fish which despite their size can be handled on light tackle provided you have plenty of line on the reel. A 20lb rod matched to 16–18lb line is about right. 300yd on the reel should give a safe margin.

The normal trace is a running leger with 2–3ft of 60lb wire for the tope's teeth to chew against. An extra 6–8ft of 60–80lb nylon absorbs the chafing from the tope's

71

sandpaper skin. Often a very long trace of 20ft or more improves catches, and this is controlled by keeping the sinker in your hand as you pay out the bait into the tide. When the desired length is reached, trap the sinker with a quick release stop knot.

A 6/0 O'Shaughnessy hook carrying a side of mackerel is quite big enough for tope but if dogfish are a nuisance they can sometimes be deterred by stepping up to a 9/0 and a whole mackerel bait.

As always, trot the bait away from the stern. There is no need to hold the rod, but by so doing you can feel if dogfish are munching the bait. Either have the reel in free spool with the rachet on, or if the tide is too strong leave it in gear with the drag just tight enough to resist water pressure.

A typical bite shows as a screaming run followed by a pause as the fish swallows the bait. Then comes a second, usually slower run as the fish moves away. Hit the tope as soon as the second run develops. Once you have caught a few, you might like to try hitting them after 15–20 yds of the first run. More are lost this way but gut-hooked tope become a fish of the past. Hit fast-running fish by braking the spool with your thumb so that the tope hooks itself against the tightening line. Once the fish is secured, let it continue to run. Big tope are impossible to stop dead no matter how strong the tackle.

In deep water especially, tope do not always make a run. The bite is a series of hard knocks like those of an overgrown dogfish. Tighten up and hit them after a few good pulls, and the tope will be liphooked. Play her as if she were a big cod.

BLACK BREAM

Despite their short season and localised distribution, black bream are such a sporting fish that many anglers travel to Sussex and Hampshire in spring just to fish for them. From midsummer until autumn the big shoals break up and scatter along the entire Channel coast and they are seldom fished for deliberately.

In early season, black bream come to spawn on a number of reefs along the South Coast. The Kingmere Rocks, Selsey Ledge and other areas of mainly chalky ground are well known. Water is generally quite shallow, tides brisk and the bottom distinctly rough.

Bream are active fish, prepared at times to feed well away from the bottom. Your bait must be positioned accordingly. Use an end tackle designed specifically for bream which enables you to switch depths to maintain contact with the shoal. The trace is long and light, the hook a fine wire 4–6.

Bream prefer long thin strips of squid or cuttlefish nicked through one end so that they work well in the tide. Similar strips of herring and mackerel are equally good at times. Worms do catch fish but are too attractive to the masses of pouting and wrasse that usually live on bream ground.

The bream population seems to be at a low ebb just now, so most days he is a lucky and skilled fisherman who takes a decent bag. You need to fish light, perhaps down to trout spinning tackle, and to carry a range of small leads so that the sinker is very closely matched to tide flow.

(Opposite) Another saltwater fighting fish. Tope hooked in deep water lack the smoothhound's speed, but are much stronger. Tope over 50lb are relatively common and a 70-pounder is on the cards in some areas like the Thames Estuary.

Black Bream from Sussex.

Drop the tackle until it taps bottom, lift the lead, tap bottom again, lift and so on until your bait is 50–60yds behind the boat. If there are no bites, rewind – slowly for the first 10–15yds – and repeat the exercise. Bites vary from gentle pecks to savage self-hooking runs. The latter bites generally ensure that the fish is securely hooked or cleanly missed. Allow more gentle bites a few extra knocks before you strike.

Bream fight with remarkable verve and determination for such a small fish. Their speed, stamina and agility makes them wonderful opponents on light tackle. Fish swimming on their sides are usually well beaten . . . but some make a last minute crash dive away from the boat.

SPURDOG

Although spurdog are common fish and caught throughout most of the year, they are at their peak in spring. Vast shoals pack together in deep water well offshore. But they do stray into shallows if enough food is there. It is then that staggering catches are made.

Depending on tide and water depth it may be necessary to use a wire line rig. Mostly, though, ordinary 20–30lb boat tackle does nicely. Spurdogs are easy to catch on just about any terminal rig, but if quantity is the aim use a three hook paternoster tied with 80lb monofilament. Change it when the line is frayed. Alternatively, a simple leger with a short wire trace is effective; and because this way you hook fish one at once, the rod and reel can be lighter. 4/0–5/0 O'Shaughnessy hook armed with smallish fish baits allow early striking and fast fishing. Bites are confident and persistent, very hard to miss unless you strike far too soon.

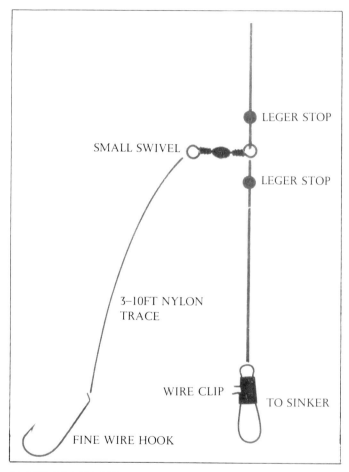

LEGER STOP

SMALL SWIVEL

LEGER STOP

3–10FT NYLON TRACE

WIRE CLIP

TO SINKER

FINE WIRE HOOK

BLACK BREAM RIG

8 Fishing on the drift

Fishing from a drifting boat is an important method although it tends to be of localised use. Normally, it is employed against fish that are widely scattered or those actively feeding on small fish and demanding a bait or lure on the move. Sometimes it is a natural consequence of the ground: pinnacle rocks · swallow anchors; featureless ground with widely scattered shoals of fish must be searched in detail.

Boats that regularly drift over productive ground – mainly offshore marks – often have extremely sophisticated electronic fish finding aids including colour video fishfinders. In the right hands these are very useful although the capital investment is mirrored in the charter fee. And, even with the aid of electronics, setting up a drift is a highly skilled job, the skipper assessing the effects of wind and tide on the boat and positioning her to follow the desired line. Adverse winds can make drifting virtually impossible if it is necessary, say, to run along a gully. An overstrong wind blowing in the right direction can also be a problem, pushing the boat along faster than is desirable.

Learning to fish on the drift is a similar exercise to bottom fishing. Look, listen and copy. And, again, it is the skipper's job to find the fish and show you the ropes. While the principles of fishing are essentially the same whether you fish bottom, drift or boatcast, the day-to-day mechanics of each branch of sea fishing have their own peculiarities. Species of fish hunted on the drift as opposed to at anchor respond better to altered rigs and modified techniques. In this chapter we look at the major drift tactics as they relate to the more common species.

PLAICE AND FLOUNDERS

Although, in general, flounders favour a mud bottom and plaice one of sand or shellgrit, they are often caught together. Thus, fishing methods are identical. The water is seldom more than 30ft deep, and the bottom is quite friendly.

Both these flatfish suffer from an excess of curiosity and the way to catch them is to appeal to it. Something as simple as a sinker dragging the bottom, sending up puffs and spurts of sand, is enough to bring them homing in to investigate. Various attractors may be used in front of the bait: coloured beads, buttons and silver foil do well. One of the best attractors is a baited spoon, either the traditional flounder spoon or a wobbling icefishing lure like the ABU Rauto.

Given shallow water and a slow drift – and the latter is vital for this kind of fishing – an ounce of lead should be enough to maintain contact with the bottom. The shadow of the boat must be alarming to fish, so let out enough line for the tackle to drag some 30yds behind the boat.

There is a lot of bumping and dragging on the road tip when the boat drifts, yet the lively pluck of a biting flatty is

Plaice, like all flatfish, react strongly to movement. Baited
spoons often catch fish when other tactics fail.

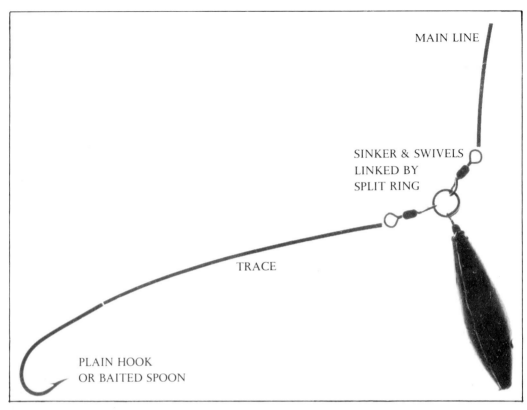

MAIN LINE

SINKER & SWIVELS
LINKED BY
SPLIT RING

TRACE

PLAIN HOOK
OR BAITED SPOON

DRIFT RIG FOR PLAICE ETC

unmistakeable once experienced. Flatfish will keep pace with the bait, tugging all the while, and it is important to allow plenty of time before striking. A hook with an offset point seems to put more fish in the boat. Size 1 or 2 Aberdeens suitably modified with pliers are perfect.

A good flatty, plaice especially, puts up quite a fight on the right tackle, making repeated dives for the bottom. Rather than haul your fish straight from the sea, use a landing net. There is little more vexing than to lose a 2lb plaice as it swings towards the gunwales.

COD

Summer cod on the drift are a different proposition from winter fish hooked from an anchored boat. Except in northern areas, they move well offshore into deeper water where the temperature is stable and low enough for their liking. In clear water conditions cod are active, aggressive predators which feed on sandeels or other small fish. At such times can great catches be made.

Pirking is the killing method, and although not everyone's cup of tea it is well worth mastering. For reasons not understood, cod seem to take pirks far better if they are worked vertically rather than dragged along the seabed, which normally means you must use no-nonsense lures weighing up to 28oz depending on speed of drift.

Pirking demands the use of a fairly stiff, powerful rod, especially so if you fish a team of lures above the pirk. Some may argue that this smacks of commercial fishing but there is no question that it works. Good lures include plastic squids in a range of colours, Redgill and other sandeels, rubber eels, feathers and Mylar lures. Hooks must be big and strong, O'Shaughnessy 6/0 at least.

The pirk itself must be armed with substantial hooks. A strong cadmium plated treble at least 8/0 is the usual choice. It may look enormous but even a modest cod will engulf it with ease.

Pirking is a simple technique but physically wearing over the course of a long day. Let the line down until the lure taps bottom. Throw the reel in gear, wind in a foot or so, then begin a gentle sink and draw action. A lift of 2ft at the rod tip is usually enough; an exaggerated action is often counter-productive. Many beginners catch more as their arms get tired for this very reason. Cod usually work close to the seabed (a good sounder shows exactly where they are) and it pays to keep the gear down there with them. Tap bottom every so often to make sure your pirk is still close to the ground.

Cod hit pirks ferociously and are almost invariably firmly hooked. The normal style of pumping a fish by raising and

Shark on! The ultimate challenge in North European waters.

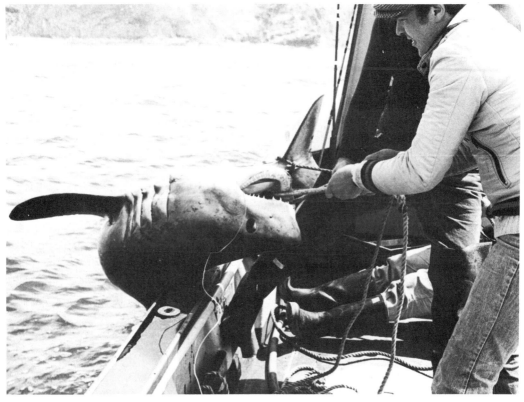

A big porbeagle comes aboard. Stand back and leave everything to the skipper. Your interference can be dangerous.

lowering the rod tip gives some problems with pirks because if the line slackens at all the pirk snaps downwards under its own weight and may dislodge the hooks. To avoid this, crank the fish up with a low geared multiplier or even a single action drum reel.

SHARKS

Porbeagle and blue sharks are the only species common to British waters. A few threshers show up most years, and the explosive mako is now a rarity. Blues are caught well offshore in the West Country, Wales and Eire, whilst the porbeagle is widely distributed and sometimes ventures close inshore. Best known hotspots

are the north Cornwall coast and waters south of the Isle of Wight.

Drift fishing with a rubby dubby trail is the way to catch both species. Rubby, the uninitiated might like to know, is a gruesome concoction of mashed or minced fish, bran and pilchard oil often pepped up with an admixture of diced fish and other smelly items that may appeal to hungry sharks. Two or three mesh bags full are hung over the side of the boat and replenished as necessary. The result is a rich, oily scent trail that spreads for miles downstream of boat and baits. An excellent rubby dubby trail is important for success, literally the essence of sharking.

The trail usually draws plenty of mackerel around the boat, and they can be feathered for bait and to boost the rubby dubby itself. This wholesale blood bath must provide a substantial extra attraction for the sharks.

Sharks are normally tackled on a float rig although some anglers like to freeline at least one bait at midwater or thereabouts for porbeagles. Various floats are pressed into service but balloons are the most common. Inflate them to the size of a grapefruit. Sharks play with the float itself on occasion, bumping them with their snouts and sometimes chopping them up. For this reason link the balloon to the main line with a length of nylon rather than hitch it directly on.

Large mackerel is the usual shark bait but sometimes two smaller ones are used together on the hook with more success. As an alternative, one or two live mackerel can be liphooked and will sometimes decisively outfish dead ones.

Two or four rods can be set up depending on the size of the boat. Typically, one float is set for 30ft and drifted 25yds from the hull; the second is set at 50ft and fished 40yds out. Rods are propped securely with

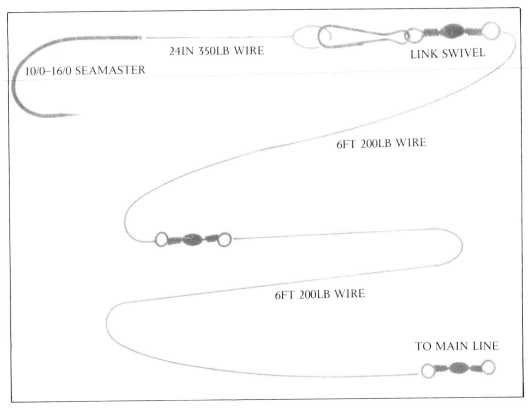

24IN 350LB WIRE   LINK SWIVEL

10/0–16/0 SEAMASTER

6FT 200LB WIRE

6FT 200LB WIRE

TO MAIN LINE

SHARK TRACE

reels either in free spool, rachet on, or if necessary with the drag slacked off enough to prevent line being pulled off by drift pressure.

Most bites come as a long screaming run. Pick up the rod, switch off the rachet and let the fish run against just enough thumb pressure to prevent backlashing. The fish stops to turn the bait, and immediately afterwards sets off again. That is when you hit it.

On light tackle of 30lb class or less, shark are struck by tightening down on the run as hard as you can. Even though line may be running out there is enough tension in the tackle for the shark's own momentum to sink the barb. With heavier gear a fish can be held much harder; three or four hard tugs ensure a good hookhold. Shark jaws have an iron grip and it is common, especially in light tackle work, to have the bait ejected after playing an apparently well hooked fish for some time.

As soon as the run starts, every other rod must be retrieved to prevent tangles during the fight and to prevent the fish snatching a second bait. Playing a shark is not too difficult if you keep cool. Do not attempt to drag a fresh fish close to the hull; it may well dive underneath and cut your line on the keel. Set the drag so that it releases line when the rod is pulled down to its full test curve – you should have checked that setting beforehand. If in doubt, err on the cautious side. A slack line can easily be tightened but a broken line is final. A big fish that runs far from the boat can be

followed if you make sure line does not fall slack as the boat gets under way.

Sharks are a scarce asset better released at the boatside. Lifting them even carefully may cause severe internal damage. Instead, leave them in the water and snip the trace with long handled pliers or disgorge the hook if it is set close to the lips. In most cases, you can leave all that to the skipper whose directions must be followed to the letter during the closing stages of the battle.

TOPE

As fully paid up members of the shark family, tope also like rubby dubby trails and at times can be a real nuisance to sharkers. However, fished for specifically from a drifting boat they offer fine sport especially on light tackle and small sinkers. You can float fish, shark style, but tope usually prefer to feed on the seabed so it is more productive in the long run to groundbait with pieces of diced fish the size of pineapple chunks and to present the hook bait on a simple bottom rig.

Lower the tackle until you feel bottom, then reel back a few turns of line. Tap bottom every few minutes in case the boat drifts over deeper ground; conversely, raise a dragging bait. A smallish bait like a mackerel fillet is adequate for this style of fishing and has the great advantage that the bite can be hit quickly with a good chance of making contact.

(Opposite) A big Isle of Wight tope that grabbed mackerel bait drifting in a rubby-dubby trail.

9 Reef and sandbank fishing for conger eels, plaice and turbot

Pinnacles of jagged rock thrust towards the surface of deep water. In holes and crevices along the lower levels of the reef, conger eels hang motionless digesting the victims of a night's hunting. Concealed under a ledge, a colony of ballan wrasse wait for crabs to scuttle within easy reach. Ling, cod and bull huss patrol slowly through the maze of gloomy canyons.

Sand swirls in a gully as a turbot rises from its hiding place to grab a small fish, one of many grubbing on the seabed. Shoals of pouting and whiting skirt a deep depression scooped out by the tide. Higher up the walls of stone, pollack resplendent in burnished gold and green, cruise slowly in the silent world ever watchful for a meal. A group of red bream, their huge eyes adapted to cope with poor light, dash through a narrow gap to another part of the reef.

A cathedral of rock rises to within four fathoms of the surface. In a valley between peaks where thick kelp sways, bass hold station to wait for a new run of tide that will turn them into ferocious predators. Here is the turbulent sound of water meeting obstruction. A fresh wind whips up a 2ft swell; steel grey water reflects a narrow path of gold light as the sun rises. A small flotilla of boats moves steadily across the horizon. The inhabitants of the reef will soon be under attack.

Areas of rock in varying depths of water are the habitat of many species of fish. A reef provides shelter but it is still very much a world of eat or be eaten where only the big and strong survive. Tidal movement has a big influence on a predator's feeding urges. A reef may appear devoid of life when the tide is slack. Succulent baits can lie within inches of ling, pollack and conger yet remain untouched. But as soon as the tide begins to move, fish stir from their lethargy and the hunt for food begins. In essence, there is the secret of fishing: being in the right place at the right time. The man who studies the underwater world and applies that knowledge to sound angling techniques always comes out on top.

REEF CONGER EELS

Congers are the biggest and toughest of reef species. 60lb specimens are not unusual. Successfully to bring such fish to the gaff demands good tackle in the 30–50lb class. A 2ft trace of 100lb wire is connected to a 7/0 to 10/0 hook, usually an O'Shaughnessy. The sinker is tied to a swivel with

(Opposite) Reef conger – a mean beast.

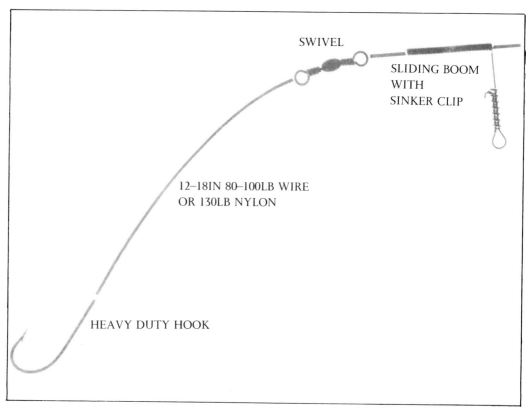

CONGER TRACE

light nylon or fished on a link leger, Clements boom or Kilmore boom. Absolutely fresh mackerel and squid are the best bait. The emphasis is on fresh – nothing but the very best will do for this species.

Most conger are slow feeders. After coming upon a bait they mouth it for some considerable time before swallowing. When you feel the initial bite, slack off a few feet of line. Hold the rod with the reel out of gear and line controlled between forefinger and thumb. Wait for the bite to develop, then wind in the slack until you feel the eel's weight on the rod. Now strike hard and winch the eel from the seabed before it has time to dive into a crevice or to grab a tailhold. Once anchored to the bottom, a conger is impossible to shift.

TURBOT, PLAICE, BRILL AND DABS

These are premier reef species, widely distributed. The best fishing is usually around the south and south-west coasts of the English Channel and sometimes in Scottish waters. Principle catches are made at the Shambles, Varne and Skerries banks where underwater dunes rise steeply to within a few fathoms of the surface and are swept by fierce tides especially during spring tides which occur around full and new moon.

Sandeels abound and are a vital link in the food chain of flatfish. The lesser sandeel and the greater species, or launce, are both prime targets for flatties, and you can be sure that when sandeels are shoaling good fishing is close at hand.

Serious fishing begins in spring when plaice move on to the banks in vast numbers. Sport can be hectic: it is common for six anglers working a mark on the Skerries to hook fifty fish on a single tide. The Skerries, offshore of Dartmouth, has become the Mecca for flatfish anglers. Rarely does the main season end without at least a couple of fish heavier than 8lb and dozens in the 6lb class having been caught on rod and line. The average plaice is about 2lb, an excellent specimen by anyone's standards.

Plaice take baits cautiously, and you must really feel for the initial bite. Light, sensitive rod and total concentration from the angler are a prerequisite. The ability to detect that first gentle pluck on the bait calls for experience. Once the bite is apparent, let out enough line to remove all tension from the terminal rig. A few seconds later the plaice, suspicions allayed, usually makes a determined attack. Resist the urge to strike too early.

Turbot, the most prized of all flatfish, are less numerous. This reef predator with a huge hinged mouth lies buried under a layer of sand or shingle with only its eyes

Electronics—quickest and most accurate method of surveying the sea bed and locating marks.

showing. There it waits for the tide to sweep food into range. Turbot attack with unbelievable speed: within two seconds the fish can dash a couple of feet, engulf the victim and be back in its ambush.

A turbot can weigh over 25lb and will use the full strength and surface area of its body in the fast tide to strain your tackle. Bringing a big fish to net can be tiring; and, of course, there is a limit to how light one can safely fish for the species. Holding bottom with the terminal rig is another important consideration for success with turbot and with the brill, another sought after species similar in many respects to turbot but smaller and, these days, even scarcer. Consider them as one so far as methods are concerned.

Terminal tackle must be fished hard down on the seabed. Rigs that lift the bait several feet into the tide will achieve very poor returns. Wire line, being of low water resistance, allows much lighter sinkers than would be necessary with ordinary nylon monofilament and brings an opportunity to continue fishing through the fiercest stages of the tides. However, the majority of charter skippers and private boat owners who specialise in reefs and sandbanks prefer to fish on the drift whenever possible.

A knowledge of the seabed is essential. Echo sounders and graph recorders locate the peaks, gullies and obstructions so that a drift pattern can be calculated. Three drifts over a series of banks usually are enough to establish whether fish are in the area. If they are not, the boat is moved 30yds to one side and a new series of drifts begun. In the course of an hour a large patch of bottom can be thoroughly worked. Of course, once the fish are pinpointed that spot is given special attention before the boat moves on.

In recent years there has been a dramatic swing to ultra light tackle for catching flatfish. Many dedicated turbot and plaice hunters now prefer an 8ft double handed spinning rod matched to a small levelwind multiplier reel loaded with 10–12lb test monofilament. The next step up, for big fish in difficult waters, is 12–20lb class conventional boat rods and reel.

Terminal rig is a 15ft monofilament trace fished in front of a weighted boom. Several types of plastic and wire booms are available from your tackle shop; alternatively, thread a Wye lead directly on to the main line behind the trace swivel. For drift fishing, a small barrel or ball weight can be set about 2ft from the Aberdeen hook so that the bait better traces the contour of the seabed. Otherwise, you lose valuable fishing time while the tackle re-settles after leaping over the sand ridge. The need to keep the bait on the bottom cannot be over-emphasised.

Turbot hit a bait without preliminaries. The first jerk on the rod tip is followed an instant later by a very satisfying curve as the fish dashes across the bottom propelled by the undulating sweep of its tail fin, which in the case of a 20 pounder is nine inches across. Hit the fish twice, and the fight is on.

Sandbank hazards are few, so fish can be given their heads. If the drag is correctly set to match the line's breaking strain, steady but unhurried pumping eventually brings the beaten fish to the surface. The fish will hang some 20ft astern of a boat anchored in moderate tides. Now is the most dangerous moment: there is a chance that the trace has been chafed by the turbot's jaws; perhaps the hook is held by the thin elastic skin in the fish's maw and risks tearing free. The trick is steadily to draw the fish towards the boat and into a wide landing net.

(Opposite) A specimen sandbank turbot.

10 Dinghy fishing tactics

Most anglers dream of owning their own boats but the regular incidence of 'nearly new' outfits for sale suggests that some at least find it a discouraging experience. In reality, a boat of your own is economical only if you make frequent use of it. The angler who fishes once or twice a month is better off on a charter boat.

Owning a boat involves constant fixed expenses. For a start, there is probably at least £2000 of capital tied up in the outfit, a sum which could be earning enough building society interest to finance a dozen charter sessions a year. Add mooring or marina fees, engine servicing, insurance, general maintenance . . . the cost soars. These fixed outgoings alter little whether you fish once or a hundred times a year. The more you fish the cheaper each outing becomes. Of course, cash is not the only consideration: there is much satisfaction in a good bag of fish won entirely by your own efforts. Once again, the more often you fish the more you learn and the better the results.

Never forget the dangers faced by small boats. Make a mistake and you may need to call out the lifeboat; you could also be dead. Anglers drown in boating accidents often because they took unnecessary risks by setting out in bad weather, in overloaded or unseaworthy boats, without local advice, without life jackets.

Boat buying lies outside the scope of this book, and in any case is absolutely dependent on local conditions and practical experience. It makes sense to join a dinghy fishing club where you should find a wealth of knowledge on all aspects of boating and fishing. Some clubs even run safety checks on members' boats annually before licensing them to fish club competitions. Fishing close by other small boats also offers the chance of a friendly helping hand if needed without having to put out a general Mayday.

You need to learn to handle your boat so well that it becomes second nature. Basic chart reading, navigation and engine repairs must be mastered. Safety equipment must include an alternative power source: oars for a 14ft open dinghy, a modest outboard for a bigger planing hull. Include life jackets for all on board, compass, baler and distress flares, first aid box and tool kit. Contact the local coastguard who will provide a mass of useful and informative literature.

Good marks can be found several ways. Some are almost universally known; club members are usually happy to pass on scraps of information especially if you have information of your own to trade with them. And, of course, you can reason out your own fishing marks with the aid of an Admiralty chart.

Dinghy anglers' navigation is fairly basic, and it is no surprise that many popular marks are within spitting distance of buoys that Trinity House so thoughtfully provides. (Never tie up to a buoy – it is illegal.)

Otherwise, locate your mark with cross bearings from known landmarks or by running a compass course at known speed and time. The latter is full of pitfalls for the

Fishing with a dinghy club, you will be safer, quicker to learn, and richer because of shared facilities.

unwary as allowance must be made for wind and tide, but with experience your calculations will come pretty close. When you are in the right general area to fish, a good echo sounder is of major assistance in deciding the exact spot to anchor.

Maintaining a log of your trips, successes and failures helps enormously in building a store of knowledge that would otherwise be forgotten. Gradually, you will find that a pattern develops; and since fish tend to hold to the same migratory routes and feeding grounds year after year, that pattern is likely to hold good at least until trawlers or pollution wipe out fish stocks or damage the food chain and environment.

Most of the techniques used in dinghy work are identical to those used in big charter boats and are detailed elsewhere in the book. But there are a number of options, mainly light tackle tactics, that are virtually unique to small boat fishing either because a 30ft boat would scare the fish or because six or eight anglers fishing together suffer endless tangles.

TROLLING

This is the art of towing a bait, usually artificial, behind a moving boat powered by oars or motor. Many outboard motors are temperamental at low speeds so an electric trolling motor could be a better choice. It is silent except for slight

91

propeller disturbance and, of course, it is not prone to oiled up plugs.

Mostly, trolling is a summer/early autumn exercise for predators feeding off the bottom: bass, pollack, coalfish, mackerel, garfish and scad. Pollack and coalies are sought after over reefs where they shoal; other species may turn up anywhere they can find food. Headlands, tide rips, harbour mouths and bays where baitfish can be herded are all good, though some marks are dangerous for the unwary boatman.

Fish feeding on fry are usually close to the surface while resident pollack and coalfish lurk around the rocks and pinnacles of the seabed. The slower the boat travels, the deeper the bait sinks. The same principle applies if you use a heavy sinker. And the more line you let out, the deeper you fish regardless of trolling speed and tackle weight.

Baits should run at least 50yds behind a power boat. 100yds is better for species that are easily alarmed. The classic formula for surface feeding bass is little lead and long line.

Dozens of lures to choose between make life unnecessarily complicated. Most

Boat, motor, trailer and accessories represent a major investment. Are you sure it is worthwhile?

8lb bass from the sandbanks. This is dinghy fishing at its best.

fishermen look no farther than a selection of Eddystone, Redgill and Delta sandeels. As a rule of thumb use natural colours of brown, blue or green for shallow work; dark shades of red, orange and black are more effective in deep water.

Avoid steering your boat through tight turns which cause the lure to lose way and sink. Steady speed and easy turns are the way to do it. The rod needs a firm rest for security; many trollers use a length of alloy tube clamped to the gunwales or transom into which the butt slides. Bites are usually fierce with the fish hooking itself, then the engine should be thrown into neutral and the boat allowed to drift while the fish is played. If you are near dangerous water and the fight is prolonged, drop anchor. And when trolling

with oars, make sure they are tied to the boat!

Baited spoon fishing is a minor trolling tactic. The style is reputed not to work everywhere, but along the South Coast at least it is by far the best way to hook flounders from April until mid-October. The special spoon lure is baited with a tough bait like king ragworm or black lugworm and is trolled very slowly behind a small pulling dinghy. Flounders swim along harbour and estuary channels with the current, tending to follow the strongest currents, so it is essential to troll *with* the tide. The spoon is fished 20–30yds astern usually at midwater or lower, but there is no need to insist on bumping the bottom. Flounders come up a long way for baited spoons and sometimes will snatch

Inshore plaice caught on the baited spoon, a technique especially suited to small boats.

them from the surface of 30ft of water.

You will notice the steady beat of the rotating spoon on your light rod tip. If it stops, the spoon has probably picked up floating weed. Bites show as a series of plucks. Just keep rowing until the rod tip arcs over, then give a hard pull on the oars to set the hook. Flounders fight well on light tackle, repeatedly diving for the sea-bed. Plaice and even bass take baited spoons on occasion.

SPINNING

Spinning involves casting and retrieving an artificial lure from an anchored or drift-ing boat. As a method it covers less ground than trolling and is generally used to catch fish breaking surface or working a res-tricted area. It is not so good for prospect-ing on the off-chance of contacting a shoal. Typical spinning marks are around headlands and rocky outcrops, alongside wartime defence works like those in the Solent and the Thames estuary, and around tide-scoured sandbanks. Aim the drift to pass clear of the edge of the shoal but within easy casting range.

The most consistent spinners for salt-water fishing are slim and silver spoons like the German Sprat, Toby and their imi-tators. Freshly killed and frozen sandeels spun on flowing traces can prove at least as good as an artificial and are a better choice over rough ground where you expect to lose several sets of gear during the day. At times it can be important to match lure size to baitfish length. On the other hand, if baitfish are excessively small, a big lure like the Rapala plug sometimes provokes a wild attack. Perhaps fish see it as a com-petitor homing in on their patch.

Baited flounder spoons can be worked from a stationary boat positioned over a known feeding ground or in a crossroads situation where two or more channels meet. Remember, the cardinal rule always to work a spoon with the current. Fish out every cast to the last few inches of line because bites often arrive as the spoon rises to the surface.

DRIFTLINING

This is a delightful and deadly technique used to present a bait off the bottom usual-ly to predatory species. Depending on the strength of tide and preferred fishing depth, you may need a spiral sinker for easy changing with variations of tideflow, or even no lead at all.

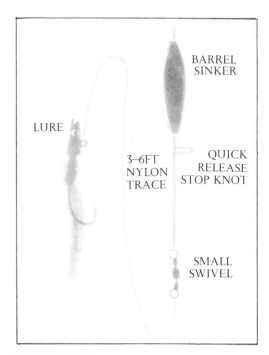

TROLLING RIG

The fish you seek in the tide run are feeding on free-swimming creatures, so it is little use to offer an inert bait like lugworm or shellfish. Top baits for driftlining are live sandeels, prawns, small fish and king ragworms. All should be hooked lightly on fine wire hooks so they swim naturally.

The bait is lowered over the side and allowed to drift downtide. Regular groundbaiting helps attract fish to the vicinity of the boat, and bites are usually confident and positive, leaving it necessary merely to tighten the line and pull the hook home.

FLOATFISHING

Floats offer the chance to present baits in a natural manner at accurately controlled depths. And, as a secondary consideration, watching a float is to many anglers the most pleasant way of all to fish.

Floatfishing is most killing for the surface and midwater predators but when the water is shallow and the tide strong enough, it can be deadly for black bream and most other species willing to rise a little way from the bottom to intercept a moving bait.

The water depths involved generally require a sliding float rig, and it is essential to make appropriate depth adjustments as the tide ebbs and flows. With a typical 9–10ft spinning rod which most sea anglers use for float work, a depth of 30ft and range of 30yds is about the limit for effective striking.

Just lower the tackle and let it drift away on the current. Control the line so that it does not belly out too far. Sometimes, holding back the float for a few seconds triggers a bite as the bait momentarily rises in the water. The trick may

catch fish when orthodox trotting fails.

As always, baits with natural movements score well. Live sandeels, prawns, small fish and king ragworm are good; a sliver of silvery skin cut from mackerel or garfish can be a useful alternative.

Float and spoon is a specialised tactic that involves trailing a normal flounder spoon beneath a float. The spoon is set to fish within 18in of the bottom, and tackle is cast uptide as far as possible so that it drifts back past the boat and on downstream. Obviously the rod and reel are held all the time so that the angler can control line which otherwise might sink or belly. The technique catches plaice and flounders but its application is limited. However, where it does work it can be devastating. Sometimes it catches fish when all other methods fail.

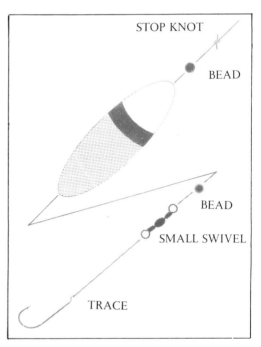

FLOAT RIG

ULTRA-LIGHT FISHING

All around Britain are harbours, estuaries and even areas of open coast where water is shallow and the tide minimal. Often these marks hold good stocks of flatties, bass, whiting, garfish, mackerel, bream and even pouting.

Freshwater match anglers regularly land 3–4lb chub from snaggy rivers on 1lb lines and size 20 hooks, yet there is a surprising reluctance on the part of sea anglers to scale down their tackle perhaps to trout spinning weight or to baitcaster and 3–4lb line; perhaps fear of losing an exceptional fish deters experiment. But with sound tackle and plenty of open water even monsters can be worn down safely.

There is tremendous scope here for dinghy anglers. Ultra-light gear shows how well even smaller species can become an excellent sporting proposition in their own right. Coarse fishing has little to match the aerobatics of garfish, the speed and stamina of mackerel or the power and manoeuvrability of black bream.

Ultra-light fishing is demanding of tackle, and it pays to use first rate line or to change it frequently. There is little enough safety margin anyway, and no room for sloppy thinking. Even the terminal rig must be scaled down to match: light rods lack the power to punch home a heavy hook and very fine wire models like Aberdeen Blues and Partridge Z9A are favoured.

11 Boatcasting

Dinghy anglers have always enjoyed one advantage over charter parties. Owing to the slap and rush of tide over hull and anchor warp, big boats make so much noise and disturbance that fish in shallow water never swim into hooking range. Dinghies sit quietly at anchor, and the fish come close. Not many years ago on the prolific cod and thornback ray marks of the East Anglian coast, a dinghy would outfish a 30ft boat five fish to one. And there were dozens of prime sandbank and estuary feeding spots where bigger boats simply could not venture.

Putting two and two together, a few more adventurous skippers like John Rawle of Bradwell and Brightlingsea's John Sait figured that by casting well away from the boat, up and across the tide, their baits would lie outside the hull's buzz and clatter and thus might attract more fish. So they did – and uptide fishing or boatcasting was born. Since then it has gained an enormous reputation around Britain, even over deep water marks where it outstrips conventional methods by a healthy margin. Now big boat fishermen can enjoy all the fish-catching benefits of dinghy fishing along with greater comfort. Restricted water depth is no drawback either: shallow draught hulls allow much better access, and besides, with modern rods and reels you can always stand off 100yds and still hit the jackpot.

It is easiest to think of uptide fishing as surfcasting from a boat. Rods about 10ft long, well tuned casting multipliers, long flowing traces and grip-wired sinkers make it very easy to lob a bait up to 75yds, about the practical maximum range for party boats. Fishing with one or two anglers aboard, you can sometimes afford to wind up the casting power into the 100yds range, though in truth such distances seldom produce extra bites.

However, a note of caution: *all* casting can be dangerous in the confines of a boat, and you must learn to take great care. Even if you avoid hooking somebody, there is a risk of the sinker smashing into a radio antenna or some other expensive target. Some skippers ban boatcasting for that reason alone. The drill is to suspend the sinker and hook outside the gunwales before flicking the tackle away with a simple overhead thump.

Uptide charter boats are no different from other party craft, and sometimes they fish similar ground for the same species of fish. Only after the boat is anchored and your mates set up their casting tackle might the truth dawn – that traditional outfit you bought yesterday is simply not right for the job. The rod is too short for casting, the reel backlashes every cast. Even the terminal rigs and sinkers are wrong.

The cardinal rule, then, for newcomers to boat fishing who live on the east coast of England, especially from Lowestoft south to the Thames estuary, is to check beforehand whether your chosen skipper is an up-and-downer or a uptider. Better still, rely on borrowed tackle until you know the score. All the best boats carry adequate tackle which is yours for the day at no extra charge.

Heavy bag of cod and bass caught by uptide tactics aboard
'Boy Carl', the renowned Brightlingsea charter boat owned by
Alf Barnard, skippered by John Sait.

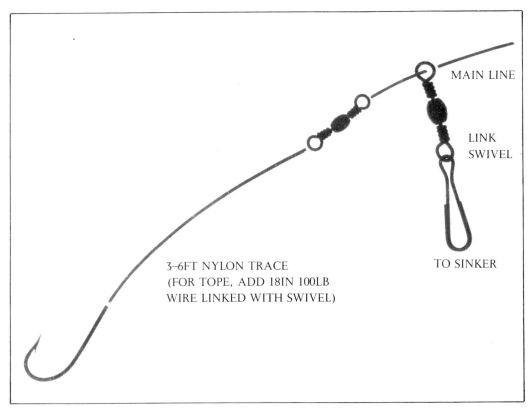

RUNNING LEGER

MARKS AND SPECIES

Classic uptide marks are sandbanks, rips, channels and gullies swept by shallow but fast-running tides. On some offshore sandbanks, a combination of spring tides and opposing wind stir up so much white water and breakers that you can almost believe you are back ashore fishing a surfbeach. It isn't as dangerous as it seems – the boat is anchored well back from the rough stuff, and you use your tackle's casting power to drop baits in the right spot.

During spring and winter, the majority of uptide boatmen concentrate on the vast run of whiting and cod that invade their territory. Fish do tend to hug the lee of sandbanks, and on occasion will hunt the very shallowest patches. But more often the shoals run through the channels and underwater creeks that crisscross the sands and open ground. Fishing tactics are thus more aligned with traditional boating practice, but still it pays to cast at least 50yds. Cod in 50ft of fast water will veer away from the hull's wake – and most cod waters are less than 30ft deep.

Late spring and early summer see a shift of scene from the open water back to sandbank tide rips where bass feed in the crashing waves that sweep small fish, crabs and sandeels downstream. A juicy ragworm drifting and wriggling downstream through wild water is a prime target for this silver flanked battler that uptide fishermen consider to be the greatest prize of all. Sandbank bass rarely top the 12lb mark, but even in these days of commercial overfishing there are enough 6–10 pounders around to ensure even the rawest beginner a fair crack at the specimen lists.

Thornback rays lurk in the quieter water around the underwater hills and sandbanks that typify uptide country. They play the waiting game, lying buried in the sand ready to snatch crabs, fish and crustaceans washed towards them. Uptiding techniques are killing for thornbacks because here again is a species that will not tolerate too close an approach by a big boat ploughing through shallow water. Ordinary boat tactics are a waste of time. But standing off and lobbing chunks of fresh herring and mackerel on uptide gear produce quite the opposite effect. It is quite common for an uptide team to boat thirty fish on a tide. Sometimes it is too easy – hence the need for conservation policies in the hardest hit regions.

RIGGING UP FOR UPTIDE CASTING

Heavy or light, boatcasting rods and reels are rigged and handled the same way. Begin by loading your reel comfortably full with 15–18lb main line, being especially careful not to raise line level on the bigger models so high that you cannot cast properly. Your thumb must wrap strongly around the reel for complete control. Make sure the spool spindle is lubricated with car engine oil, and either insert medium brake blocks or dial maximum magnet setting. This basic tuning ensures against backlashed casts.

Tying a sinker directly to thin main line guarantees cracking off the terminal rig

first cast. Instead, uptide fishermen use a shock leader of 20–50ft of high-test monofilament inserted between rig and main line. The shock piece absorbs casting pressure and is also useful when you haul a big fish towards the hull. In effect, your tackle becomes 30–50lb class during those final hazardous feet as the fish thrashes into gaffing range. Attach the leader with a Figure Eight/Uni Knot combination, and, above all, make sure there are at least six full turns of leader on the spool when the terminal rig is suspended ready for casting.

Running legers are par for the boatcasting course. Most experienced fishermen use nothing else. First, slide a link swivel on to the leader. Thread on a bead, then tie a second swivel to the end of the leader. Now attach a monofilament trace that will vary between 2 and 6ft long depending on where and when you fish. On average, a 3ft trace of 15–25lb line fits the bill. The main exceptions are summer bass, which can safely be tackled on lines down to 12lb, and big thornbacks which soon chomp through traces flimsier than 30lb. Although wire traces are never required for ray fishing, you do need the extra insurance of heavy duty nylon to buffer the ray's teeth and skin. In fact, uptide men use wire only for tope fishing, and even then they prefer to restrict it to the final 12in. The rest of the flowing trace is tied from 35–50lb monofilament which shrugs off abrasion from the tope's sandpaper flanks.

Hooks for boatcasting are generally the same as those used for all-round boat work, but it makes sense to choose the finest wire and sharpest point compatible with the species you aim to hook. Striking at longer than normal ranges, you certainly need all the penetration you can get. Excellent hooks include Breakaway's Spearpoint Boat, Mustad Vikings and, for run-of-the mill codling and whiting, Mustad Aberdeens.

Counteracting tidal current is quite a challenge. Most of the time you must ensure that once it has hit bottom, the tackle stays put. If it skids downtide, it sweeps under the hull or tangles with your neighbours' lines. Either way, the whole principle of boatcasting is defeated. The simplest answer is to take another tip from beachcasting – use a wired bomb sinker with fixed or swivelling anchor spikes. On the whole, swivelled wires are the better bet because they do not restrict retrieve. However, fixed spikes do seem to resist the tide a little better and sometimes become necessary on big spring tides that scour through deep cod channels.

HOW TO ANCHOR YOUR TACKLE UPTIDE

Lob your baited tackle uptide and away from the boat, then brake the spool to a stop as soon as the sinker hits the surface. (If you do not stop the reel, the line will backlash in a flash.) *Immediately* release extra slack line into the current, controlling the reel with your thumb. Give *plenty* of slack line – 25yds if necessary – before flicking the reel into gear. Now the line pulls tight against the current, drives the grip wires deep into the seabed and holds the bait steady and well uptide. Water pressure strains the rod tip over, so you must either tie the rod down, or, better still, keep hold of it. *Important*: the system will not work if you immediately tighten down. All that happens is a steady drift downstream across other tackle.

Fish hunting with the tide seldom play with the bait. Cod, bass and whiting rush in, snatch the hook and run off. The impetus of their attack rips the grip wires out

of the seabed and line falls slack. The rod tip bounces back in a positive reaction that nobody could mistake.

You have one priority: reel in the slack line and make contact with the fish. Wind as quickly as you can until you sense the weight of the tackle, then lift the rod high. Keep the pressure on and pump the fish towards the boat.

Taking in the slack sets the hook. More important, you contact the fish while it is still uptide of the hull. Thus you fight it downstream to the boat, which is much easier than to battle it uptide against the current. The bigger the fish, the more difficult it is to pump against the tide without straining the line. Be particularly careful with rays which open their wings like a giant kite and sometimes 'fly' to the surface many yards downstream of the boat. Sheer weight of water on a 10lb thornback ray is enough to snap 15lb line.

THE ROLLING LEGER

The rolling leger is arranged in exactly the same way as standard uptide gear, but the spiked lead is replaced with a plain bomb. It is a valuable rig for summer fishing for bass in white water. The skipper moors the boat in deep water ahead of the rip, then you cast a rolling bait across the tidestream so that it trundles into the shallows. Keep hold of your rod, and be ready to strike at the slightest bite. Mostly, though, white water bass attack viciously, hook themselves then run for the breakers. Hold the rod tip high, take your time and, above all, make sure the reel's drag is preset. Uptide bass never need a second chance to break free.

*Hit your fish hard, reel in the slack, and pump the fish inboard
before it can drift too far astern.*

12 Wreck fishing

The seabed around Britain is a ships' graveyard. Hulks are a haven for fish of all kinds and sport is spectacular. Wrecking is synonymous with outsize specimens, and dozens of records have been set since the sport began in earnest in the 1960s.

The vast numbers of fish caught in those pioneering days from inshore wrecks by anglers and commercial fishermen could not be sustained. Today, top flight charter skippers routinely sail many miles from port to locate new wrecks with enough good fish to satisfy the specimen hunters. The main centres for wrecking are Brixham, Plymouth, Mevagissey and Whitby which all have reasonable access to thousands of virgin wrecks lying in rich water. Yet sometimes it is still necessary to steam for 50 miles. Wreck fishing, then, is not for the fainthearted or for anglers looking for low cost entertainment. Fees are high, the necessary good tackle is expensive, and long hours at sea are physically taxing.

Offshore wrecks can be found only with electronic equipment. Charter boats are fitted with Decca Navigator, a sophisticated radio direction finder which compares three crossbearings transmitted from shore with an accuracy down to 12ft. Even in fog or at night a skipper can set his Decca co-ordinates and steer a precise course for a distant hulk. Once over the wreck, he switches to an echo sounder.

The sounder sends a signal into the water through a transducer in the boat's hull. The electronic pulse travels to the seabed and bounces back, and these return signals are electronically decoded and displayed on graph paper or a video screen. A very accurate picture of the wreck and its surroundings build up: modern equipment is able to recognise shoals of fish, individual fish, even plankton.

Anchoring to or drifting over a wreck requires a great deal of skill. Anglers who ship with leading skippers owe their vast catches to one man's seamanship. Wind, tide strength and sounder interpretation also play an important role. The biggest catches are made during the middle-range tides which allow fishing at anchor. At other times the run of water is just too much and even 2lb of lead are swept away so powerfully that no angler can touch bottom in 40 fathoms.

Drift fishing is the alternative style effective for pollack, cod, ling and coalfish; but even they take refuge behind rusting ironwork when the tide runs its hardest. Spring tides virtually rule out conger fishing except during the brief spells of low and high slackwater. In short, study the tide tables before you book a wrecking trip. Also consider whether you are up to an expedition.

Top line skippers with large boats equipped for long voyages tend to make light of

(Opposite) Wreck fishing calls for endurance and sheer muscle power. Big ling like this do not give up without a hectic struggle.

The catch rate on a virgin wreck is phenomenal. Your party could boat 2000lb in one session.

weather that others consider more than rough. The possibility of having to endure long hours on a constantly lurching boat with saltwater coming over the gunwales and rain driving down should be carefully considered. Not every trip is like this, but a fair percentage are close to it.

To be well clad is very important. Temperatures offshore are very different from those on land. Wind blowing off the sea can be chilling and damp, and without adequate clothing the body cools rapidly. Cold is a prime inducer of seasickness.

One-piece waterproof suits with hoods are the best protection; some are classified as flotation suits and will hold you afloat should an accident occur. In everyday use any good suit keeps out the wind, maintains body warmth and fends off the rain for hours on end.

Underneath go cotton trousers and a wool sweater over a thick shirt. Cold feet make for a miserable day, so wear insulated socks and a decent pair of short rubber boots with non-slip soles. Woolly hat and gloves complete the outfit. Unless it is a summer day with no wind and sea like a millpond, put the suit on before you leave harbour because it is all too easy for a wave to come over the side without warning and soak you to the skin.

FISHING THE WRECKS

Conger, ling, pollack, coalfish and cod are the principle quarry of serious wreck fishermen. All the current British records were set on hulks lying between 20 and 50 miles offshore. The biggest black and red bream also were hooked from wreck marks, and at least four record weight turbot have been landed on baits aimed at conger. The big flatfish take up residence in hollows scooped by the tide at the side of a wreck, and some skippers deliberately anchor off-centre of the wreck for a while just in case there is a monster in hiding.

Discipline is important when drift-fishing a wreck. If the boat's complement is ten anglers, only half of them can fish comfortably from one side of the craft, which drifts beam-on. Those on the 'wrong' side must fish under the boat, an extremely unpleasant and often downright difficult experience. To compensate, most skippers work the drift turn and turn about so that each side of the boat gets an even chance of fishing correctly.

Drifting with a well-weighted paternoster made from 80lb nylon monofilament carrying two snooded 8/0 hooks is a technique that pays off during the winter when the heaviest concentration of ling and pollack invade the deep water wrecks. Hooking a pair of ling together weighing 60lb or a brace of pollack at 18lb each is not uncommon, hence the need for strong arms and first rate tackle.

A variety of natural baits are used, but the trend is towards artificial squids, nicknamed muppets, and pirks. Large 20–26oz models fitted with a treble hook are preferred and are often baited with squid or mackerel. 30lb class stiff-actioned boat rod and fast retrieve multiplier matched to 30–40lb monofilament line is the correct combination for this style of wreck fishing.

The terminal rig is dropped quickly towards the bottom. Sometimes the lures are hit long before the tackle reaches the wreck because during the colder months predators swim in shoals at varying depths, quite often high above the pile of junk. However, should the rig hit the seabed it is wound clear of the wreckage and jigged.

After setting up the drift, the skipper watches the sounder. When the end tackle

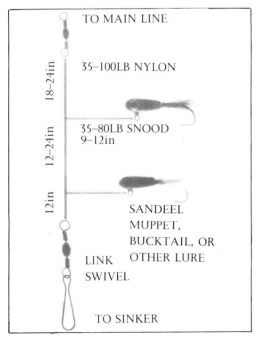

TO MAIN LINE

35–100LB NYLON

18–24in

35–80LB SNOOD
9–12in

12–24in

12in

SANDEEL
MUPPET,
BUCKTAIL, OR
LINK   OTHER LURE
SWIVEL

TO SINKER

HEAVY DUTY PATERNOSTER FOR LURES

almost touches the wreck, he shouts instructions on how far to wind in. Delay results in the expensive trace tangling in the superstructure. As soon as the danger is past, down go the pirks and muppets close to the lee of the hulk where lies the heaviest concentration of fish.

Fishing at anchor requires the boat to be a considerable way uptide of the wreck so that falling baits land close by or actually inside the hulk. The anchor is dropped according to the tide's angle and strength. Precision is essential, and sometimes several attempts are needed to hold the boat in exactly the right spot. The distance between anchor and wreck is seldom less than 300yds.

Fishing for specimen pollack is highly specialised work. Most of the largest fish are caught on marks in the western Channel where they live throughout the year. However, winter sees the record breakers coming over the side. Monsters over 20lb figure strongly in wreck catches.

Although many are hooked by anglers fishing heavy duty paternosters, the flying collar featuring a very long trace up to 20ft is a far better proposition. It is worked from a wire boom that prevents the trace tangling the reel line.

The collar is made up by attaching split rings to all three corners of the boom which carry swivels and a swivelled weight holder. The reel line of 15–20lb monofilament and the trace are then connected. The weight carrier allows the sinker to be changed quickly to suit tidal conditions.

4/0 hooks are the most popular and may have feathers whipped on for extra attraction, a refinement often used by pollack fanatics who spend their waking hours thinking about this hard fighting, highly entertaining species.

Mackerel strip, squid and king ragworm are preferred natural baits. Artificial eels, usually 177mm size, are deadly for the species and should be stocked in a variety of colours. What works one day may not be as good on another; artificial eel fishing is largely a matter of experiment.

The flowing trace is dropped to the bottom and then retrieved slowly. Pollack prefer a moving bait, hence the necessity to keep the reel turning even after a take is detected. Counting the turns of the reel handle is an easy way to assess the level at which the shoal is feeding. If several pollack are hooked at forty-five turns, the lure can quickly be retrieved almost that far next cast, saving time and wasted effort. It is a trick that adds many fish to the bag in the course of a day.

Flying collar rigs are dependent on a good run of tide which streams the trace and gives the lure a natural swimming action. It is a useless rig during neap tides and slack water. However, used at the right time it is a deadly technique for pollack and coalfish as well, and no serious angler can afford to ignore it.

Wreck fishing for conger eels has long excited anglers. There is something special about hunting a species that grows to 10ft long and a weight of 150lb. The British record stands at 109lb 6oz but much bigger fish have been brought close to the gaff, and huge fish were netted commercially. It is a fish of mystery and imagination, and will remain so.

Conger are nocturnal fish, most of them becoming very active only after dusk

(Opposite) Conger – fish of mystery and imagination, and one of the few species that feeds better at night.

settles. On a gloomy wreck in deep water, competition for food is intense and eels may feed during daylight as well. However, the most hectic fishing is enjoyed by anglers lucky enough to hit the wrecks all night or just before dawn.

Wreck eels are nowhere near as cautious as eels that live on reefs and broken ground. They attack baits presented on 10/0 hooks snooded to a short wire trace or to commercial weight nylon. The trace is rigged on a running leger with 30–50lb class rod, reel and line. The rod is hand-held with the reel in gear.

An eel indicates its arrival with a series of hard knocks. Pay out a few feet of slack line to encourage the conger to take the bait – usually fresh mackerel, squid or a small fish such as pouting. After a short wait the reel is engaged and loose line reeled in. If the eel has taken the bait it will back slowly away; you can feel the fish's weight as the line tightens. Hit it hard two or three times to sink the hook, then reel and pump the fish away from the wreck. You must haul an eel into clear water before it has time to realise its danger and run for the ironwork. Once there, it would be impossible to shift.

As soon as the eel is safely above the wreckage you can afford to slacken the drag and let the fish battle it out. Most big eels make four or five fierce dives for the seabed, and though the reel must be set to pay off some line you still cannot afford to give an extra inch of slack. If necessary, hold the conger very hard indeed even at the slightly increased risk of snapping.

An 80lb eel is a formidable opponent capable of regaining 40 fathoms of line with an unstoppable dive. Yet with care even the biggest of eels can be brought safely to the gaff. Then your troubles really begin. Daylight drives a conger mad and it fish spins like a top or backs away shaking its massive head. Always guard against that last dive for safety.

Boating the fish is the skipper's responsibility. He will not thank you for getting in his way. The drill is to draw the fish to the side of the boat, throw the reel out of gear, and stand back. Now the skipper has room to swing the fish inboard with one smooth lift of the gaff. You must resist the temptation to see what is happening. And do not be too anxious to drag the eel within gaffing distance in the first place: outsize fish that are not worn out can be dangerous to gaff.

Other fishing books published by The Crowood Press

Imitations of the Trout's World *Bob Church and Peter Gathercole*
Natural history, physiology, distribution, tackle, tactics and techniques are
discussed in this most comprehensive study of the species.

Handbook of Fly Tying *Peter Gathercole*
A guide, in full colour, to tying a wide range of flies, with every step
illustrated with a colour photograph.

The Complete Boat Angler *Bob Gledhill*
A comprehensive guide to the when, where and how of boat fishing.

Fishing with Bill Sibbons *Clive Graham-Ranger*
Clive spent a year fishing with Bill Sibbons to produce this account of the
man whose ability to take big trout from small waters has become legendary.

The Beach Fisherman's Compendium *John Holden*
A guide to long-range casting which also covers rods, reels, accessories and
rigs.

Beach Fishing *John Holden*
An introduction to tackle, casting and the bait needed to catch the more
popular sea fish from beaches.

Quest for Barbel *Tony Miles and Trefor West*
The most complete handbook on barbel fishing ever produced.

Fly Fishing for Salmon and Sea Trout *Arthur Oglesby*
The first really comprehensive work to deal almost exclusively with fly-fishing
techniques.

**Tactical Fly Fishing for Trout and Sea Trout on River and
Stream** *Pat O'Reilly*
An in-depth look at this most mobile form of fishing.

Pike – In Pursuit of *Esox lucius Martyn Page and Vic Bellars*
The most complete book on pike fishing, both in Britain and abroad.

Big Carp *Tim Paisley and Friends*
A selection of stories and much advice on how to catch carp over 25lb by
many of the top men in the sport.

Trout Angler's Angles *Alan Pearson*
More thoughts, ideas and advice from one of the best known trout fishermen.

To Rise a Trout *John Roberts*
A highly acclaimed handbook giving practical and authoritative advice on dry-
fly fishing on rivers and streams.

Trout on a Nymph *John Roberts*
Campanion to *To Rise a Trout* which looks at subsurface fishing for trout.

Waddington on Salmon Fishing *Richard Waddington*
The latest thoughts from perhaps the greatest salmon fisherman of the
century; full of thought-provoking ideas.

Further information from **The Crowood Press** (0672) 20320